War in the New Century

Other titles in the New Century series:

War in the
New Century

Jeremy Black

Continuum
London and New York

VNYS UA 700 .B497
2001 c.1
KGQ020E-2005

Continuum

The Tower Building
11 York Road
London SE1 7NX

370 Lexington Avenue
New York
NY 10017–6503

www.continuumbooks.com

© 2001 Jeremy Black

All rights reserved. No part of this publication may be reproduced or transmitted in any form or by any means, electronic or mechanical, including photocopying, recording or any information storage or retrieval system, without prior permission in writing from the publishers.

First published 2001

British Library Cataloguing-in-Publication Data
A catalogue record for this book is available from the British Library.

ISBN 0–8264–5164–0

Typeset by Kenneth Burnley, Wirral, Cheshire.
Printed and bound in Great Britain by Biddles Ltd, *www.biddles.co.uk*

Contents

Preface

In the closing decades of the twentieth century, there was much talk of the obsolescence, not to say the end, of war. Arguments varied, but a combination of atomic weaponry, a declining interest in both conquest and military service and the supposed weakness, not to say collapse, of the state combined to lead to such claims. If war was outdated for these reasons, it was also, in a separate analysis, presented as pointless because of the overwhelming military hegemony of one nation, the USA, the leading economic and scientific power in the world. The notion of a Revolution in Military Affairs (RMA) was advanced in order to describe changes in the nature of military power and, in particular, both the technology of force and force projection, and the likely character of future warfare. In specific terms, there was an emphasis on information as a force multiplier, as well as a measure of military capability, and also as an objective in war: 'degrading' the information systems of an opponent was seen as the way to victory. As the USA monopolized the cutting edge of this technology, it was seen as being a paradigm leap ahead of possible opponents.

In this book I take a different view. Throughout, I intend to try to take a global perspective, rather than a Western one. This will differ from most works on war: these are very much Eurocentric in character, inclined to take the Western state as a norm, and likely to focus on technological triumphalism.

I will argue that the notion of the so-called 'revolution in military affairs' that sees 'smart' weaponry as the driving force in war and military capability is wrong, because it fails to note the multiple contexts of war, not least differing understandings of victory, defeat, loss and suffering. In short, war and success in war are cultural constructs. In addition, these constructs interact with socio-political developments. So, for example, democratization, changing gender relationships and the resurgence of religion as a focus of identity and loyalty in much of the world are more important than cruise missiles and other new weapons. Democratization has sapped willingness to accept conscription, while feminism, changing gender relationships and the role of women in armed forces are important in the decline of bellicosity in the West.

These will be the themes of Chapter 1 which will be taken forward into the rest of the book. Chapter 2 focuses on civil war; the rise of civil conflict and the decline of the state monopoly of force in given areas. This decline has international consequences, not least as collapsed or weak state forms, for example in Lebanon, Sudan and Congo, interact with international hostility.

Chapter 3 looks at the difficulty of sustaining systems of international agreement and mediation. Thus, in contrast to the claims of those who proclaimed a New World Order of democratic capitalism after the fall of the Soviet Union, there will be an argument that such ideas reflected not a prospectus for the future, but a degree of Western confidence and global influence in the 1990s that could not be sustained, not least because of the rejection of Western norms in China and much of the Islamic world. The chapter will also address the issue of future conflict between the USA and China, and between the West and the Islamic powers. In the latter case, it is important to note the continuing role of religion in provoking or inspiring war, and the Western, secular perspective that 'doesn't get' religion on its own terms, and therefore both fails to understand the motivations behind 'religious war' and is ill-equipped to negotiate exit-strategies for these types of conflict. The issue of 'rogue states' will also be considered; it is important both in its own terms and for what it says about the problems created for the West by the failure of the world to conform to Western norms.

Chapter 4 picks up from there and looks at what fighting and weaponry are likely to be like in the future. Particular weight will be devoted to the interaction of, and differences between, land, sea and air capability and conflict. In the Conclusion, in place of the 'revolution in military affairs' approach, I will focus on the revolution in attitudes to the military and on the limitations of the technological approach.

I have benefited from the opportunity to lecture on future war in my 'War and the World' course at Exeter University. This has provided a stimulating and friendly environment for the development of ideas. I would also like to thank David Hayden for his helpful comments on an earlier draft of this book, and my son Timothy for valuable comments on the science of future soldiery. If this book leaves the reader, like the writer, feeling pessimistic, I hope that it is at least a more informed pessimism. I will be delighted to be proved wrong.

For Gigi and William Salomon,
with thanks for their friendship and hospitality

1 War Today

> It could be argued that the American Civil War inaugurated a
> system of warfare that, among the sophisticated, industrialized
> powers, has run its course.
>
> Brian Holden Reid, *The American Civil War* (1999)

Writing in 2000, it is difficult to credit claims that war is obsolescent. Furthermore, such claims appear not only ludicrous, but also worrying, a complacent echo of similar assertions made prior to World War I, when Western powers dominated the world and traded with each other, and when systems of peaceful international arbitration were discussed. It is of course true today, as it was a century ago, that war can seem irrational. A cost-benefit analysis of conflict rarely favours war. This has become even more the case as the interconnectedness of the global economy has gathered pace. In a world of globalism, war truly can appear dated, for it depends upon a degree of autarky or self-sufficiency that is incompatible with the assumptions of the political economy of the modern world, with its stress on the free flow of trade and investment. However, such a policy of autarky, or at least of protectionism, may seem crucial to the maintenance of particular interests threatened by this political economy.

Furthermore, there is a long tradition of wishing that war was anachronistic, a savage throwback to a former primitive state and/or an aberration on the course of human and societal development that can be overcome. This was given eloquent form on 3 September 1939 when Britain entered World War II in response to the German attack on Poland, and George Lansbury, the pacifist former leader of the Labour Party, told the House of Commons:

> The cause that I and a handful of friends represent is this morning, apparently, going down to ruin, but I think we ought to take heart of courage from the fact that after 2,000 years of war and strife, at last, even those who enter upon this colossal struggle have to admit that in the end force has not settled, and cannot and will not settle anything. I hope that out of this terrible calamity there will arise a real spirit, a spirit that will compel people to give up reliance on force, and that perhaps this time humanity will learn the lesson and refuse in the future to put its trust in poison gas, in the massacre of little children and universal slaughter.

A belief that peace is natural and necessary, in the past, the present, the future, or all three, can be used to make war appear as unnecessary.

Yet that does not necessarily make war anachronistic. Indeed, the very frequency of war over both the last century and also the last decade suggests that it is unhelpful to regard it as an aberration. This is particularly the case in areas where conflict has been frequent such as the Middle East. If 'war' is considered to include civil conflict and international quasi-wars then it can be seen as normative in many regions, indeed possibly the normal state of human society. Such an approach would see periods of peace as being periods of 'inter-war'. While literally true, this is a somewhat glib comment, that provides no guidance to the extent to which peace is becoming more prevalent. One of the themes of this book is that war seems less normative and less normal in the Western world as the bellicosity of populations declines, but that this is not the same as a fall in the frequency or impact of conflict. The apparent disjuncture of these two developments can throw much light on a world that at once can appear more peaceful and yet be more violent.

There are particular reasons for an increase in tension and violence, aside from the general prevalence of violence as a means to pursue interests and assert identity. It can be argued that globalism (and other characteristics of the modern world) itself accentuates the possibility of conflict. Globalism does so for three reasons. First, the nature and pace of links within a globalized world create strains, especially in terms of economic pressures and living standards, that throw up a violence of 'counter-globalism'. This is readily apparent in the Islamic world. There, 'counter-globalism' can be seen as a defence of values, and these living values are not rendered suspect to local opinion by being traditional.

This potent rejection is directed not only at the international forces of globalism, especially multinationals, and foreign borrowing, their institutional structure, such as trade pacts and the International Monetary Fund, and their alleged global standard bearer, the USA, but also at local élites that are identified with this world. Hostility to globalism in many states means opposition to modernism and modernization, and thus can draw on powerful interests and deep fears.

Secondly, and conversely, the definition of states or groups that fail to conform to the international order and political economy of globalism, so-called 'rogue' states, leads to pressure on the stalwarts of this global order to push them into line, either because of their domestic policies or their international stance, or both. If this leads to military action, such a policy can be, and is, presented as policing and peace-keeping, but the reality is war. Indeed, the very willingness to consider, plan for and execute military schemes that are presented as peace-keeping suggests that war in that guise has become a ready response by liberal Western powers, such as the USA and Britain, that do not consider themselves authoritarian. In the future, war in this guise may become a more common and widespread response to international disputes. In particular, it may be as difficult to restrict the self-selection of peace-keepers to those who currently dominate 'peace-keeping' as it is to prevent the diffusion of weaponry from advanced states.

This device of making military action appear more acceptable by defining it as peace-keeping is thus potentially

destabilizing, and could cause war by emulation. This is particularly the case as the global pretensions of peace-keeping are not
matched by any marked effectiveness on the part of international institutions. Thus, the ability of the United Nations to
define peace-keeping and the peace-keepers and, therefore, to
legitimate and de-legitimate war is limited. Within some states,
there is an analogous problem as militarized peace-keeping by
armies and police forces is rejected by some of the population,
while the state authorities lack the legitimacy of consent.

Lastly, the very nature of a global economy is that it is both
dynamic and prone to bring the far-distant and different into
contact. This is destabilizing. Thus, experience and expectations, 'real' interests and assumptions combine to make
globalism a cause of conflict, however much this conflict undermines the logic and profitability of globalism, not least by
introducing a powerful element of instability.

In addition, aside from the issue of globalism, even if war is
anachronistic for some, many or most states and interests, this
does not mean that it is, or appears to be, for all. In short, it is
mistaken to argue from the general to the specific. In many
senses, indeed, the course of both international relations and
military history are the revenge of the specific on the general
(and the generals!).

There are many groups that have found conflict welcome,
and that will continue to do so. It can seem the best way to
pursue interests, not least if these are 'revisionist' (designed to
reverse a past settlement). Furthermore, conflict can have a
cultural, emotional or ideological appeal that those who do not
share these assumptions or attitudes find difficult to appreciate.
It can also be the salve for boredom or a sense of cultural ennui.
In the past, this has encouraged a sense that war was a valuable
cure for national ills, an attitude that continues to have more
vitality than is sometimes realized.

Far from seeming anachronistic, war, defined as the use of
organized force, in the first eight months of 2000 was the

solution both of 'developed' states and of their 'less developed' counterparts. The former case included the Russian invasion of the breakaway state of Chechnya in the Caucasus and the British intervention in civil war in Sierra Leone. As far as actions by 'less developed', or less powerful, states were concerned, it was possible to cite a number of conflicts, including those in Zaire and Angola – both civil wars – or the war between Ethiopia and Eritrea. These were not minor struggles; indeed, all three involved substantial forces, as did the Sri Lankan war with the separatist Tamil Tigers. Furthermore, civil wars on this scale have a capacity to draw in other powers. It is commonplace to accuse neighbours of sheltering rebels and to demand rights of pursuit; furthermore, refugees pose a major problem for neighbours. Whatever the response by neighbours, the struggle can spread. Namibia allows the Angolan government to operate in its territory against the Angolan UNITA rebels, thus leading to UNITA reprisals. Zambia refuses, leading to tension, including Zambian claims of Angolan forces crossing the frontier.

It would be misleading to segregate 'developed' and 'less developed' states because, aside from serious problems of definition with the term 'developed', it was also the case that 'developed' states tended not to fight each other, but rather to employ their forces against the 'less developed'. Thus, aside from taking direct action in the Caucasus, the Russians in May 2000 threatened air strikes in order to prevent Afghan support for insurgents there. Similarly, the long-standing conflict in the southern Lebanon between Israeli-backed forces and the Islamic guerrilla Hizbollah movement abated when the Israelis withdrew the same month, but it is possible that this conflict will resume.

The current tendency of 'developed' states not to fight each other is not necessarily some lasting rule or guide to the future. Aside from direct conflict, they can fight or compete for influence through surrogates. This was very much the case in the Cold War, for example in the Middle East and Central America.

It can also be seen in recent struggles, for example in Africa and the Caucasus, although the extent to which this is the case is a matter of dispute. For example, it is not clear how far the civil and international wars in Central Africa, particularly in Rwanda and Congo, should be traced to French policy, as has been alleged. It was also claimed that British or 'Anglo-American' interests lay behind Rwandan and Ugandan intervention in the Congo, but this has been denied. The extent of Russian involvement in conflicts involving Armenia, Azerbaijan and Georgia in the 1990s has also been a matter of controversy.

It is necessary to understand war as a very diverse process. This has obvious implications for any analysis of conflict and, more generally, for the assessment of military capability. If wars are different, and military tasking, therefore, very varied, then it is unhelpful to think in terms of a single hierarchy of military capability, however that hierarchy is arranged, or to argue in terms of a narrow range of military characteristics.

Currently, such a hierarchy is generally arranged in terms of military technology, particularly weaponry – although there are also other aspects of technology, especially those related to command and control functions, transport and logistics. These are all important, but a focus on the material culture of war – weaponry and weapons systems – is only useful if it is con-textualized by an understanding of the very varied character of war and of the extent to which superior technology does not necessarily bring victory, let alone success.

The latter is a lesson taught by military history, both distant and recent, and thus provides an opportunity to underline the importance of such history for an assessment of conflict and capability today and in the future. Such an assertion may appear anachronistic and, indeed, military history, on the whole, plays a smaller role in military education today than was the case a century ago, although the situation varies by country and service: air forces tend to be less interested in military history than armies and navies. (This owes something to the shorter history of air forces, but more to the cultural assumptions of those who go into the service.) Instead of considering past conflict, more time in military education has to be spent evaluating the consequences of technological advances for war at the tactical, operational and strategic level.

Not to do so would of course be foolish. It is important to use weapons effectively and to triumph in engagements. However, a wider understanding of the capabilities of military forces requires an assessment of conflict that brings out its multiple and unpredictable character. This can be glimpsed by looking at military history. There are many instances of this, of which the most prominent in recent decades is the unsuccessful American intervention in Indo-China in 1963–73. The latter is an extensively debated conflict, and there is much contention in particular about how far the American failure was due to the inherent difficulties of the task, and how far it was due to problems in the USA, ranging from an eventually critical media to excessive and/or unfortunate political interference in military policy. It is not the purpose of this book to re-examine the war, but current debates are part of the military world of the present day and will help shape future assumptions. In one respect, the reluctance by many who discuss the Vietnam War to accept the limitations of technology, especially air power, and the search for failure at home is the most important aspect of the debate, for it has obvious implications for how future conflict is considered. Indeed, future war can be used to fight out different interpretations of the past.

On the global scale, it can be argued that the technological optimum, in terms of relative military capability, that appeared apparent in the late-nineteenth century, receded in the second half of the twentieth century; and that conflict today, and in the foreseeable future, can be located in terms of this process of the erosion of military effectiveness and success stemming from technological advantage. As this is an important point that underlies much of the analysis in this book, it requires some explanation. Let us start with visual images, which have become more potent than for our predecessors because of colour and the incessant presence of film and television. The visual image of war on the global scale in the nineteenth century was of Western supremacy. Close-packed lines or squares of Western infantry were depicted shooting down large numbers of non-Westerners, both infantry and cavalry, who hurled themselves towards the disciplined firepower of the Westerners.

As with many images, this, in part, described a reality. There were battles like this, such as the British defeat of the Mahdists at Omdurman in the Sudan in 1898, and there was an overall capability gap. However, there were also engagements where Westerners were less successful. Their weapons were useful, but issues of terrain, ecosystem, tactics, leadership, morale and unit cohesion were also important. In addition, weapons themselves were spread to non-Westerners, for example helping Ethiopia defeat Italy at Adowa (Adua) in 1896; while, anyway, the advantage provided to Western forces by individual weapons could be lessened by the adoption of particular tactics by opponents.

All of these factors ensured that the situation in the nineteenth century was more complex than is sometimes appreciated. In addition, it is necessary to consider military operations within a wider political context in which Western imperialism both appeared normative to Westerners and could benefit from circumstances elsewhere, not least from the ability to win local co-operation, as in India and Nigeria. This context helped empower the Western military capability referred to, and should not be separated from the more narrow military analysis.

In the twentieth century, the politics of power changed. This undercut whatever military advantages the Westerners possessed, and also altered their use in particular circumstances. The politics, however, were the crucial change. Imperialism not only ceased to be normative in the West; it also became unacceptable to those who were under imperial rule. These developments were related. They also did not arise at a particular moment but instead were a shift that occurred over much of the century. This shift was the context within which military capability has to be judged. In short, political will is not a constant.

This shift is not stopping in 2000, nor due to stop in the foreseeable future. Indeed, in many respects, past, present and future are all linked here because it is unlikely that, in the foreseeable future, we will move towards a situation in which imperialism is seen as desirable and acceptable. This anti-imperialism is a fundamental building block in the military situation because military capability is in large part set by objectives, or 'tasking'. In other words being 'fit for purpose' is a key aim for the military, but purpose is constructed in terms of particular political circumstances, both domestic and international. This is true whether the military is subordinated to civilian political control or whether it is autonomous, or even in control of the state.

Political circumstances have changed profoundly. Indeed there has been, and will continue to be, a Revolution in Attitudes towards the Military (RAM) that has had a profound impact on the objectives and conduct of military operations and the nature of military institutions. This revolution has focused on a decline in the willingness to serve in the military, both in peacetime and in war. The causes of this vary by individual, but they can be summarized in terms of the movement towards societies that are more individualistic, and towards a culture that is more hedonistic. Other '-isms' of the recent past and the present that are relevant include consumerism, capitalism and feminism, as well as democratization. They are each more powerful because of their interaction.

Feminism is particularly important, because it can be argued that there has been a reconceptualization of masculinity in the West in recent decades as part of a change in gender identities and relations. More specifically, the acceptability of constructions of masculinity in terms of the ability and willingness to be violent, and to be seen to be violent, have dramatically fallen. This is important because much work on military effectiveness in combat conditions stresses the need to avoid shame in front of fellow-soldiers. As definitions of bravery and shame change, so conduct in the field is potentially affected. This is certainly a concern among opponents of the use of women as 'front-line troops'. As Chapter 4 shows, however, the notion of a front line has largely disappeared from modern Western military doctrine in favour of the notion of manoeuvre warfare, deep penetration advances, and a zonal battlefield. As a consequence, any opposition to the use of women in the front line will in practice remove them from the combat sphere.

On the other hand, it is possible that talk about the reconceptualization of masculinity refers more to 'official' culture than to general social attitudes. There are still important definitions of male identity and heroism in terms of violence, for example in film and video, especially in the USA. These frequently present violence as regenerative, and reflect a bellicosity that is powerful within Western society.

Nevertheless, the filmic images also capture an important shift in institutional values, because the heroes are often defiant individuals, loners who have to fight because of the supineness and folly, not to say treachery, of established channels of authority. In short, the discipline and comradeship of military units is not the model for modern images of exemplary violence, and these images conform even less to practices of command and hierarchical structures. A stress on interdependability, and controlled interdependability at that, that characterizes both traditional and, even more, modern concepts of military organization and conflict is not the characteristic of the lone hero, whether on film or in a computer game.

The acceptance of women for front-line units is a product of changes that result from feminism. Despite resistance in some quarters, this is likely to continue in the future, especially if fitness and other requirements can be appropriately varied, although it is important to note that in Israel, despite much myth to the contrary, women are not usually assigned to combat roles. The likely future rise in the number of women in front-line and command positions in many forces will not, however, lead to a presence comparable to men, because sexual stereotyping will continue to be important, and because positive attitudes to the use of violence will remain more true of men. Nevertheless, many weapons are increasingly designed to take note of average female, as well as male, physical characteristics.

The role of women in the armed forces will also be an aspect of future military life that will remain heavily culturally conditioned. A major role for women will be far more true of Western societies than of Oriental counterparts, let alone Islamic states; and this will be especially true of command positions. The more prominent role of women will affect the image and self-image of Western forces, although there will be reluctance and resistance.

As a related point, Western forces are also being forced by political pressure to alter their attitude to the recruitment of publicly professed homosexuals. Because covert homosexuals were always part of the armed forces, this is less important a shift than the recruitment of women for combat units. Nevertheless, it is indicative of the extent to which Western forces are no longer able to set the parameters of military culture, and, instead, increasingly conform to general social mores. Indeed, civilian control extends to the details of practice and ethos. This is further ensured by the intervention of litigation in internal military matters, a trend that is likely to continue as hitherto privileged jurisdictions are subordinated to the authority of judicial processes.

In part, this reflects the new definition of public interest in the West. In the past, such an interest would have protected military autonomy, but now, to jurists, such autonomy seems an abuse, or, at least, an anachronism, and their attitude takes precedence in government and society. It is also actively supported by media products, such as films and television, that castigate supposed military abuses, such as alleged sexism. To some within the military, the widespread acceptance of criticism and judicial intervention amounts to a situation where it can seem as if preparedness is presented as less in the public interest than the pursuit of 'politically correct' strategies. At the very least, this opens up another contrast between Western militaries and those where there is no such attempt to reconceptualize (or, to its critics, attack) military culture, or at least military authority.

The decline of conscription has been a measure of the RAM, although it is an imperfect one, both because conscription has had particular meanings in individual states and because conscription itself is not simply an index of bellicosity. Indeed, it can arise from defensive intentions, and is important in societies that stress the idea of the citizen soldier. This was true, for example, of Revolutionary, nineteenth-, and twentieth-century France and, more generally, was seen as an important way to ensure the maintenance of accountability within the military and also democracy in society. This process was very important after World War II in countries that identified a professionalized military with right-wing politics, the position in several European states including Germany and Italy.

However, this civic militarism receded at the close of the twentieth century and looks set to continue to do so. It remains important in some states, especially Israel and Switzerland, but no longer frames the military culture of the major powers, nor of many other states that had previously put an emphasis on conscription. It is readily apparent that conscription has become less acceptable in the West over the last four decades. Civic militarism was eroded by social shifts and ideological and cultural pressures, such that conscription was increasingly seen as an aspect of authoritarianism, and not as civic militarism. Again, this is a good example of the extent to which changing conceptions that are not inherently military nevertheless have a direct impact on military life and possibilities.

Furthermore, over the last four decades, a gulf widened between conscription and military professionalism, and the latter was seen as more important. The most important shift occurred in the strongest power, the USA. There conscription had been the legacy of World War II, and had been continued in peacetime during the Cold War. The Korean War (1950–53) underlined America's needs for numbers, and its consequent world-wide commitments made it difficult to abandon conscription. In addition, it very much accorded with the dominant ethos of 1950s America, an ethos that was to be greatly challenged in the following decades.

Conscription fell victim to America's disillusionment with the Vietnam War, and with practices and symbols of authority. In 1968, Richard Nixon, then a presidential candidate, announced that he would get rid of the draft, and he had done so by 1973. This marked a particularly important shift and example, as America was then at war in Indo-China, as well as having other major commitments elsewhere.

In Europe, Britain had already given up conscription, which did not have a historical purchase in its public culture, and was only introduced to fight the two World Wars. However, in most other countries, for example France and Russia, the decisive shift occurred in the 1990s, and was due for implementation then and in the following decade. The process continues. In June 2000, the Italian Parliament passed a Bill phasing out conscription by 2005. It was designed to replace an army of 270,000 with a professional service of 190,000, including women. Ivica Racan, who became Croatia's Prime Minister in 2000, is in favour of cutting the army from 60,000 to 40,000 and phasing out conscription. The Turkish army has begun to talk about abolishing conscription as part of a programme of modernization.

In states that preserve conscription, such as Germany, it was frequently discharged through social service. The special commission set up under Richard von Weizsäcker, a former President, to investigate the future of the German military, recommended in 2000 that the number of conscripts be cut from 130,000 to 30,000, as part of a cut in the army from about 340,000 to about 240,000. In addition, where conscription remains, there is no effort to extend conscription to women, despite their new-found assertiveness throughout the West.

Such a shift away from conscription can be explained by arguing that these states did not face serious military challenges, and there is much truth in this analysis. Yet, such an explanation is not the whole story, and the cultural changes already referred to were of great importance. It is also less valid for Israel, a state that has repeatedly faced war and confrontation since it won and preserved independence in 1948. However, in 2000, disillusionment with military service was presented as a reason for Israel's abandonment of its presence in south Lebanon.

In the case of Israel, and, indeed, other states where support for military service ebbed, this shift can be linked to a reconceptualization of such service. In place of the soldier as potential victim, and an acceptance of the likelihood of casualties, has come a search to banish casualty from the lexicon, and an emphasis on an offensive–defensive stance focused on technology, especially air power. Thus, Israelis became less keen on defensive positions in which troops were vulnerable, and, instead, preferred the idea of a reprisal military, essentially using the air to overcome the problems of the ground.

A move away from conscription was also an aspect of the professionalization of war that became increasingly insistent as the large citizen militaries that had fought World War II were replaced across most of the world by far smaller regular forces. This again is a sphere in which the present seems to be no abrupt barrier between past and future, but, rather, a continuation.

Professionalization was assisted by the development of a branch of the military in which manpower was not crucial: air forces. A focus on machines not manpower had always been the case with navies, although they also required appreciable numbers. However, only a minority of states were naval powers, and, as a consequence, armies dominated models and practices of military organization and culture.

Air forces offered a very different ratio of man and machine, man and killing power, man and cost, from armies. Their presence, role and aura assisted in the shift towards a more professionalized concept of war. So also did changes in land warfare, changes that gathered pace in the last quarter of the twentieth century, retain their importance today, and will do so in the foreseeable future. The ratios referred to above shifted as the effectiveness, cost and requirements on their operatives of particular machines increased. The real cost of soldiers also rose, as the low-wage jobs of the nineteenth and early-twentieth century were placed under pressure from rising wage, and other cost, rates. These were a function of growing affluence and expectations, especially in the West.

Costs per individual soldier had been held down under conscription, but that increased the aggregate cost of the system, as large numbers had to be equipped, transported, housed, clothed, fed and trained, demands that absorbed much of the budget of armies that retained conscription in the 1990s. In addition, large numbers of fresh conscripts each year had to be trained, ensuring that their forces were very much barrack armies lacking mobility. Furthermore, as these soldiers mostly left military service quickly, the long-term benefit of such training was restricted, other than in creating a large potential reserve with limited and dated military skills.

Conscription also seemed increasingly inefficient and obsolescent, because the requirements from individual soldiers rose as training requirements became higher, and training regimes became longer and more difficult in order to cope with more complex machinery. As a result, the labour market dimension of military recruitment was not that of the bottom of the market, but rather that of competition in the skilled section.

Thus, cost and technology factors combined to encourage a professionalization that also reflected social trends. In short, militaries sought to transform themselves into volunteer forces. These were seen as most likely to be truly effective, for effectiveness was seen as much in terms of morale and unit cohesion, as of equipment use. High morale and unit cohesion were regarded as important in fighting quality, as is indeed the case. It was harder to develop and sustain such morale and cohesion in conscript units. High morale and a sense of professionalism that in large part came from volunteer recruitment and long service also made it far less likely that military forces would reject or question political control and their instructions. A citizen army in the age of democratization – a period in which there are increased demands for democratic practices and institutional responsiveness – appeared undesirable to governments, militaries and citizens alike.

Volunteer service meant that the military had to find ways to attract and retain sufficient numbers of the right kind of recruits. This helped to alter the social politics and internal dynamics of military service, and was, also, related to both professionalism and improved military practice. In particular, a mutual trust of officers and men, based on a shared competence and reliability, helped to improve effectiveness. This looked towards future practice, as such a mutual trust very much became an objective of unit structures and practice. Volunteer long-term service also led to greater concern about the families of military personnel and the impact of postings on family life. Provision for families also increased the cost of the military system and diminished the ratio of expenditure on front-line preparedness.

The above comments are in part misleading because they adopt a paradigm, that of the Western army. Having warned about the danger of creating a model, and hierarchy, based on Western technology, it then is inappropriate to do the same based on a particular account of organizational development, specifically recruitment and internal dynamics. However, the processes described above are not restricted to the West. Indeed, there are important Oriental parallels. In the 1990s, the Chinese military embarked on a similar process of cutting numbers, and of professionalization and improved machinization. The three were linked, but it is too simplistic to see the shift to different machines, i.e. a new technology, as driving the system. This, however, is more possible for China than for Western powers because in China there is less need to heed popular views. A stress on regular forces, rather than on mass-armies and reserve militias, could also be seen in other leading Asian states, such as Japan and India. A million strong, the Indian military was very large, but it was small compared to the size of the population. Again, this was linked to a number of factors, not least the desire of India to appear as a regional force, and the absence of any wish to overrun its neighbours.

The differentiation between the military and the remainder of the young adult male population that volunteer service produced was less marked in countries where state authority and the practice of impartial law and order were weaker. This was true of parts of Africa and of states such as Lebanon and Afghanistan. Here, the organizational account of differentiation between armed forces raised by voluntary recruitment and civilians who had chosen not to volunteer neither conformed to long-established social patterns nor to recent political events. It is to these that we will now turn, not only because they are important in their own right, but also because they challenge any analysis of war and the military that focuses solely on state-to-state conflict.

2 War and the Collapse of the State: the Future

> The alternative to the state may not be a harmonious universal society, but fragmentation into warlordism, rule by gangs, communal massacres, and 'ethnic cleansing' . . . the major sources of war in the future will derive less from the character of relations between states than [from] what goes on within states.
>
> Kalevi Holsti, *The State, War, and the State of War* (1996)

As already suggested, in the intensely visual culture of the present, filmic images of war are the most potent, and with 'virtual reality', this is likely to become even more the case in the future. These images derive in great part from science fiction. In the account of war seen in major films such as *Independence Day* (1996) there is no comparison whatever between the two sides: one is human, the other alien. It is a fight to the finish, and the finish is destruction.

This is a basic theme in science fiction. There are films and television programmes in which alien systems seek to co-exist, for example the *Star Trek* series, but they are very much in the minority. In contrast, a depiction of other humans in terms of alien qualities and the inherent need for a fight to the finish is no longer acceptable, at least in what is generally in the West seen as civilized society. The focus in science fiction on conflict between civilizations is analogous to the idea of sharply differentiated states, but, even more, there is an emphasis on technology and on war as occurring between manned (or aliened) weapons with scant need to consider the civilian population. As a result of the focus on technology, science fiction appears similar to much of the discussion that surrounded the Strategic Defense Initiative (also known as Star Wars) plan announced by President Reagan in 1983, and, more generally, that around the current Revolution in Military Affairs (RMA).

Thus, in both the imaginative world, and in that of theorists and planners looking ahead to future conflict, there is an emphasis on the civilization/state and its armed forces as a unit actuated by technology, and as likely to be victorious as a consequence of its successful use. Most literature on the future of war would adopt this approach and be an exercise in futurology. This is not without value, for the military capability of the major states, and conflict between them, if it occurs, does change and will continue to do so. Thus, there is need for futurology. As a consequence, we will turn to this approach in Chapter 4.

However, such a perspective is far less suitable when it comes to looking at a range of conflict that in no way corresponds to the world of science fiction or 'high-tech' warfare. This range is organized around two types of war that are far from coterminous but that frequently overlap: civil war and 'low-tech' war.

Civil war is the great forgotten in military history. Such a remark might appear ridiculous given the amount of attention devoted, in particular, to the American Civil War (1861–65), and, to a lesser extent, to the British civil wars of 1642–48, but the civil conflicts that receive most attention are those, like these, that oppose regular forces to each other, and can thus readily be accommodated to the central narrative in military history. In fact, this is not the case with most civil conflicts, and will not be so in the future; and their relative neglect is a serious problem with much discussion of war.

In addition, an account of future warfare that focuses on futuristic technology has little time for civil conflict, most of which is 'low-tech'. There has been some discussion of futuristic non-lethal weaponry that would be appropriate for dealing with hostile compatriots, but hitherto it has not played a large role in most discussion of such conflict. Sticky substances and other incapacitants may be useful in controlling some riots, but it is difficult to see them as solving the problems posed by insurrection in, for example, Sri Lanka, or by terrorism in, for example, Peru.

It is probable that civil conflict will become more common. Before discussing this claim, it is worth noting that civil conflict is difficult to define, and even more so than international war. At one side, it fades off into policing. This is true of states with separate police and military forces, such as Britain, Spain and France, confronting violent separatism in Northern Ireland, the Basque Country and Corsica respectively. It is even more true of states that lack a separate police force. There, the maintenance of internal control is a prime responsibility of the military.

Again, this is a division that should not be pushed too hard. In some states, the police, or part of the police, can be described as militarized, and, in others, the challenge to ordinary policing is such that the army has to be used to maintain order.

This account sounds benign, in that the emphasis is on challenges to government and order. It is also the case, however, that in some states the prime challenge to order and good government, and indeed to society as a whole, can be presented as coming from the military itself, or from a state apparatus using force in order to maintain a control that is not answerable to the citizenry. Modern Burma and Iraq are good examples. In such states, the brutal and frequent use of the regular army, as in Burma, or of militarized forces, such as the Republican Guards in Iraq, is an aspect of politics; indeed, civil conflict is politics.

The causes and nature of such conflict vary; they also contribute powerfully to the military history of past, present and future. Thus to look to the future is, in part, to look to the pressures that will exist within states and societies, to the methods of dealing with them, and to the role and success of force in furthering strategies. Military history takes on some of the characteristics of 'total history'.

The nature and severity of the pressures that exist within states and societies have been regarded very differently over the last decade, and there is no reason to anticipate any greater uni-formity in the future. The fall of Soviet Communism led to assertions of the so-called 'end of history', and, more particu-larly, of the end of divisions that had caused international and civil conflict. Thus a double hegemony was seen: on the global scale the 'new world order' presided over by the USA, and, within states, a combination of democratic politics and capital-ist economics, both acting in a benign fashion.

Confidence in this projection ebbed during the 1990s and has not revived. It became clear that there were powerful counter-currents, not least a resurgence of religious fundamentalism and of ethnic tension. In addition, an optimistic conviction of the ability to solve disputes short of conflict appeared less convinc-ing. Conflicts in the Balkans and Central Africa, but not only there, played a large role in affecting confidence. The disruption created by global economic pressures became more apparent.

In considering the future, these factors are pertinent. In addition, there are structural changes in the world that suggest that more disputes will arise. The first relates to population increase, which provides a Malthusian vista of conflict derived from numbers exceeding resources. While it is true that birth rates in many countries are falling, and that aggregate global population growth is expected to fall after mid-century, it is, nevertheless, the case that the intervening growth is still seen as formidable. The 1999 United Nations Population Fund Study suggested a rise from 6 billion in 1999 to 8.9 billion in 2050. These figures reflect not only the entry into fertility of current children, but also improvements in public health and medical care that lead to a rise in average life expectancy, and to cultural restraints on restricting family size and the use of contraception.

This rise in population has tremendous resource implica-tions. Furthermore, these will remain the case even if growth rates slacken. This is because, aside from the rise in overall demand for employment and resources, there will also be a con-tinuation in the rise in per capita demand. Indeed, belief in a likely fall in population growth rates presupposes such a rise as it asserts a virtuous linkage of economic growth and falling population. An alternative, predicated on rising levels of fatal diseases, is not anticipated, with the exception of AIDS in parts of sub-Saharan Africa, although the disruption caused by such diseases may well be a challenge for armed forces in the future.

Rising per capita demand is seen as a function, both cause and consequence, of economic growth and development, but these themselves are a cause of instability, because, despite technological improvements in productive efficiency, they pose major demands upon available resources. In addition, irrespective of economic growth, demand rises because of important social shifts. The move of much of the world's population into urban areas will continue. This is linked to a decline in former patterns of deference and continuity, both within families and communities, and more generally. In urban areas, there is a willingness to reject parental aspirations and living standards, and an increased exposure to consumerist pressures. Such pressures, and the accompanying rejection of the past, are also present in rural areas. This reflects the role of migration, as well as the massive extension of access to television in countries such as India, and the role of advertising. The destabilizing sense of a better world elsewhere that West German television brought to East Germany in the 1980s will be repeated throughout the world. Indeed, it is not surprising that Islamic fundamentalists seek to prevent or limit the spread of information about Western life, nor that the Western model is perceived as a threat by them, indeed a form of war.

Demands for goods and opportunities will be a cause of dispute and instability in families, communities and countries. Just as higher rates of unemployment tend to be linked to crime, although this can be cushioned by social welfare, and most of the unemployed are not criminous, so a sense of poverty, whether absolute or relative, encourages alienation and a feeling of dispossession. Violence is a response, although the reasons are complex. Nevertheless, it is worth noting that in many areas affected by high rates of poverty, crime rates are rising. Thus in Greater São Paulo in Brazil the number of murders rose and remained above 6000 in 1994 and above 8000 in 1998, and, more clearly, 1999 – with the rate of murders per 100,000 passing 40 in 1994 and 50 in 1999. In some areas, such figures can be seen as a sign of a degree of social disorder that can be regarded as civil war, certainly as far as many individuals and communities are concerned. This is even more true in many states of the struggle against the drug trade which destabilizes entire societies, leading to the corruption of politics and business, and to high levels of crime and social breakdown.

At the national level, rising demands will increase the volatility in many states. This will be particularly so in those that cannot ensure high growth rates and the widespread distribution of the benefits of growth, nor dampen or control expectations. There will also be an age dimension, in that ownership of property and financial assets will be concentrated among the older cohorts of the population, and spent on their welfare, and thus will not satisfy the younger cohorts.

Demands for goods and opportunities will exacerbate problems of political management within (as well as between) states, encouraging the politics of grievance and redistribution. Conflict creates poverty, but poverty encourages conflict. As damaging is the sense of relative poverty that will be felt by those who are comparatively well off, but have not had their expectations realized. Such a condition can also be ensured if there are checks in the process of growth. Thus, alongside the urban and rural poor whose hopes for a higher living standard (in some cases a living standard) are not fulfilled, will come those who are better educated and have gained jobs, for example in the state bureaucracy, but who feel angered by the limited benefits they have, or can anticipate. This last group may include sections of the military. At any rate, anger will be directed against those apparently benefiting from conditions and at their foreign links.

As a consequence, economic growth may well not serve to assuage internal tensions. There may well be no political or ideological cohesion to the state to encourage the élite to develop policies of sharing benefits or arranging welfare provision. The resulting tensions will interact with a hostility to the élites' modernizing ideology and policies. The result will be an internal hostility, that would be prone to the outbreak of civil conflict. This could take several forms, including violence against particular ethnic groups, but will reflect the precariousness of government structures and the difficulty of developing systems of mutual benefit.

This account is more true of some parts of the world than of others. By 1999, 95 per cent of the rise in the global population was occurring in 'developing countries', in many of which the population lacked adequate housing, sanitation and health services, and were also increasingly conscious of their relative deprivation. In addition, it was estimated in 1999 that nearly a billion people were illiterate. This again increases volatility. Furthermore, there was a political 'impoverishment', in that the means to press for significant change peacefully within the political system were often absent.

The resulting politics leads to grievances and clashes over resources, both of a conventional type, most obviously land and water, and of a more 'modern' type, such as quotas in educational opportunities, housing, and government jobs, and the allocation of economic subsidies. Disputes over such issues make it easy to elicit popular support, and can make it very difficult to secure compromise. They provide the lightning rod for regional, ethnic, religious and class tensions, for example in Pakistan. The attempted coup in the Solomon Islands in 2000 arose from tension between two ethnic groups, the Malaitans and the Guadalcanal people. The Malaita Eagle Force mounted the attempt in order to draw attention to its demands. In the same year, disputes over the benefits from the drilling of oil in the Niger delta led to growing regional tensions in Nigeria.

The potential danger of such tensions is readily apparent in some countries where grievances are freely voiced within the political process and also in the media. They are also present, however, in states that make much more of an effort to suppress such expression. The most powerful of such states is China. In this state, it is unclear how far the government will be able to contain the consequences of very varied growth rates and economic conditions. Differences accelerated in the 1990s, not least with the expansion of special economic zones, and are likely to continue to do so. In part, resulting tensions have been lessened by internal migration, but there are major problems. First, attempts by the central government to benefit from growth will lead to major rifts, not least because there is a powerful regional dimension, with expansion in the south and government in the north. Secondly, the resource demands of the rapidly expanding regions, particularly for food and water, will lead to resistance elsewhere, as shortages develop and prices are pushed up. The range of possible conflict was indicated in Hunan province in 2000 as local television operators resisted attempts by China Telecom to enter the local television market with violence, that, so far, has left 100 dead or wounded.

Furthermore, the Chinese military is increasingly fractured on regional grounds, with an identification between particular units and regional interests. This is a long-term factor in Chinese military history, which reached its apogee with the warlord era of the 1920s. Communist attempts to use party control in order to overcome such fissiparous tendencies had only limited success, not least because of the difficulty of rotating army units in order to break down their regional identification. Indonesia faces the same problem.

It is unclear how far divisions within China will take a military dimension. This is important for the future of warfare, not least because of issues of scale. The largest war in the nineteenth century occurred in China – the Taipeng Rebellion – as did the largest (in terms of combatants) after 1945 – the Chinese

Civil War. It may well be that in terms of people involved, the largest war in the twenty-first century occurs in China, and is a civil war. This could be a world away from the analysis of future warfare favoured by protagonists of a revolution in military affairs.

The modern Chinese military is not well adapted for a sustained, large-scale civil war, as modernization has led it to shed the numbers that might be required to hold down a dissident population, and, for example, escort food convoys. As a consequence, the war is likely to entail the use of police forces and perhaps of militias. It will be presented to the outside world as resisting 'bandits', thus returning us to the problems of defining war.

Such disputes can also be particularly brutal. This is in keeping with the general tendency of so-called primitive warfare to cause higher casualty rates than the majority of conflicts involving regular forces. Over the last half-century, smaller numbers have been killed by bombing than in close-quarter combat. This is particularly the case with civil wars. A recent example is provided by the very high death rate in civil conflict in Rwanda, especially the Hutu-directed genocide in 1994, where many of the victims were beaten to death. Although regular forces can be vicious, they are less likely than non-regular forces to engage in wholesale slaughter of ethnic and other groups judged to present a challenge. This can currently be seen with killings within Indonesia, for example of Christians in the Moluccas. In Northern Ireland and Spain, the indiscriminate killing of civilians was a characteristic of terrorists, not of the army nor of the police.

Again, however, it would be unwise to adopt too clear-cut a distinction on this point. The conduct of the German army in World War II stands as a striking example of how a force that justifiably prided itself on its professionalism could play a role in genocide. There was not the shadow of a military reason for this conduct, and it cannot be extenuated by reference to the difficulties of holding down a hostile civilian population. Indeed, German brutality helped to encourage opposition.

Looking to the future, it is probable that fear about ethnic difference will drive genocidal policies, or, at least, the savageries of 'ethnic cleansing'. It is also possible that the problems of operating in a hostile environment will lead to brutalities directed at civilians, not least because of the difficulties of identifying guerrillas from the rest of the population.

The prospect of chaos and conflict over resources is not restricted to poor countries, nor to those with non-democratic political and governmental systems. For example, in democratic India, there is a major contrast between the forces of the central government, which include rockets capable of carrying nuclear warheads, and the situation in a state like Bihar, where the private militias of landlords, especially the Ranbir Sena, compete with Maoist Naxalite guerrillas, and the latter compete with each other. Such competition can take on the intensity of a low-level war. Inter-community violence is not easily suppressed by small, high-tech regular forces. Were more states to have nuclear weapons, the contrast would be more common.

Resource issues have, in part, been lessened over the last century as a result of economic growth and technological improvement, for example in agricultural yields which have been particularly important in enabling much of the Third World to feed itself and the First World to do so without having to use its purchasing power to take food from the Third World. However, it is by no means clear that such growth can be maintained, certainly at a high enough level to meet individual and aggregate demand. This is particularly serious in areas of rapid population growth, and, indeed, elsewhere given the ability of hungry regions to export their hunger, by importing food if wealthy, or exporting migrants if poor. The assumption that science will always provide is less sure today, as confidence both in science and in rationalist solutions ebbs.

In addition, the environmental damage of industrial society

and modern agricultural practice is increasingly apparent. Governments eager for economic growth, such as those of China, India, Indonesia and Malaysia, tend to ignore such damage, but it may indeed feed into the general picture more directly by hitting this growth and challenging stability. For example, the denuding and contamination of ground and underground water supplies is a serious problem, affecting agriculture in India and elsewhere. Like the loss of soil through deforestation and inappropriate agricultural regimes, it will cause enforced migrations.

These problems will interact with volatile domestic divisions. For example, concern about water supplies will exacerbate relations between groups practising different forms of agriculture. There will be claims that minority groups are responsible for the contamination or depletion of environmental resources, and thus for what will be presented as a form of internal conflict.

Resource problems will not prevent high levels of military expenditure. Despite the terrible poverty of much of their population, India pushed up defence spending by 14 per cent in 1999, and Pakistan by 8.5 per cent, to total allocations of $9.9 billion and $3.3 billion respectively.

Resource issues will also be a major problem for the leading economic powers. This will reflect rising real prices and also limited capability for efficiency gains through product substitution or new production techniques. While this will not be true for all products, or for all of the time, it will be sufficiently so to be an important factor. A recent precursor was the pressure in 2000 created by rising oil prices, which caused domestic political problems in a number of states, both 'Third World', such as Zimbabwe, and Western, including the USA, Britain, and, most seriously, France; though prices fell in early 2001.

There will be future instances, and they will create numerous tensions, both domestic and international. Energy costs will be a particular focus of tension, not least because of the failure of nuclear power to fulfil expectations and the absence of a sequential development in the nuclear field. As a result, the focus will continue to be on the exploitation of non-renewable resources. Rising costs will encourage the exploitation of hitherto unprofitable resources, but this process will not provide low-cost energy, and, once tapped, the resources will also be rapidly depleted.

As inexpensive and immediately accessible energy has been internalized and made normative in the assumptions of Western life, its removal will cause great stress and lead to a demand for action and a search for culprits. This will be particularly true from economically marginal groups, such as the rural poor, but such 'marginality' may extend to all those whose socio-economic position is precarious. This could include industrial workers and others threatened by global competition, and thus much of the population. A limited willingness to accept the consequences of global shifts in energy prices and the power of the state to set tax levels was readily apparent in France in 2000. The political process will channel such anxiety and anger, leading to confrontation and conflict, expressed in terms of extremist political movements, contentious internal regulation, and international dispute.

In short, resources may be the cause and/or occasion for conflict whether the state, region or social group that is the aggressor is experiencing economic growth or the reverse. There have been many accounts of why economic growth and social development will cause peace. In 1828, William Mackinnon, later a long-serving MP, claimed, in his *On the Rise, Progress and Present State of Public Opinion in Great Britain and Other Parts of the World*, that:

> the prevalence of public opinion may be the cause of hostilities between nations not being so common as in days of ignorance . . . when the individuals of those classes that most influence public opinion are aware that the pressure of taxation will be felt, more or

> less, in consequence, the community will not permit themselves,
> as in former days of ignorance or barbarism, to worry and attack
> their neighbours for mere pastime, or to gratify their caprice or
> warlike inclination . . . To argue, that because war has desolated
> Europe almost without intermission, longer than the memory of
> man or history can record, it will be as frequent in future, would be
> judging erroneously, and not making sufficient allowance for the
> present state of civilization and power of public opinion . . . As
> other nations become civilized . . . communities will be benefited,
> in general, by an interchange of commodities . . . As civilization
> extends itself, the art of war is brought to greater perfection, and
> the burdens attendant on such warfare press more heavily on the
> community . . . In an improved commercial and agricultural state,
> wars are seldom undertaken but for the sake of preserving indepen-
> dence, or of obtaining some great commercial or political
> advantage; as they necessarily tend to impoverish the community
> which governs itself by public opinion, and acts according to its
> interests: hostilities, therefore, are not likely to be undertaken
> hastily, to be waged with acrimony, or extended unnecessarily.

This comforting account left no room for ideology and politicization. In the event, the rise of commerce, industry and the
middle class was not to prevent bitter and costly wars between
'civilized' states, nor indeed the brutal conquest of much that
Mackinnon thought barbarous. One of his own sons was killed
in the Crimean War of 1854–56.

Looking to the future, it might still be argued that prosperity
and the pursuit of profit ensure that war will be unlikely for
advanced states, because the benefits of ease will be widely distributed. Such claims have indeed been made. However, it is just
as likely that the segregation of a professionalized military and
the cult of new technology will encourage the notion of a cost-
less war.

In practice, such conflict is very costly and likely to remain
so. The very essence of a modern professionalized military is

that it requires specialized equipment and support systems that cannot readily be improvised or requisitioned from civilian uses, although, especially for shipping, there have been attempts to encourage convertibility, and thus to lessen the need for specialist production runs. Nevertheless, there is greater specialization than was the case in the pre-machine age. Furthermore, as production runs have become shorter, so the real cost of military hardware has risen. As a consequence of such specialization, the cost cannot be offset by operating in foreign states, as was the case in the past.

Any sustained high-tech war would be very expensive, but it is unclear that the forces mentioned by Mackinnon would therefore act to prevent conflict. Instead, the principal domestic sufferers will be those affected by cutbacks in social welfare and by wartime inflation (for example the elderly), neither of which is generally the most 'empowered' group of members of the community.

Irrespective of this, the mechanics do not exist in crises, especially in the rapid run-ups to conflict, to allow the careful evaluation of popular views, and, in particular, of the extent of a disinclination to fight; if indeed such exists. Furthermore, foreign policy and defence are areas of policy that remain particularly under the scope of government control and in which secrecy is defended. This makes it far harder to conduct any informed policy debate, and to point out the drawbacks and unpredictabilities of conflict. This was very apparent during the Kosovo crisis of 1999. It is unlikely that this situation will change.

Resource competition is not the sole structural issue causing conflict between and within states. Another is that posed by the breakdown in the integrative capacity of states. This can be seen not only in the countries generally seen as facing problems of widespread poverty, but also in their affluent counterparts. In general, assimilative ideologies and practices have become (or, in many cases, have remained) weaker, and governments find it increasingly hard to persuade minorities to renounce violent opposition. Governments will also find it difficult to restrain their own propensity to use their authority in order to advance policies without sensitivity to the interests of sections of society. This can be a problem not only in autocratic societies, but also in democratic states that use a majority mandate to ignore minority views.

In theory, modern states will be far better able to control and suppress discontent. They will have the capacity to create a surveillance society in which the government will possess considerable information about every individual, including their location. Furthermore, the nature of the modern salaried workforce and, through social security, non-workforce, is such that most people will not be able to break away from this surveillance society. It is possible that information capabilities will grow if chips are implanted in individuals. There will be social benefit excuses, but the consequence will be to enhance the surveillance resources of government.

Aside from information, Western governments will also continue to have important resources. Their internal control forces, whether military or police, will have communications, and command and control facilities that will be greater than those enjoyed even recently. Furthermore, training for dealing with internal control, and the provision of specialized units, will both improve.

Yet, as with the emphasis on technology in international capability and conflict, such a stress can be misleading; and can also risk extrapolating to the entire world circumstances that will only pertain in part of it. Furthermore, the factors of individualism noted in the discussion of the Revolution in Attitudes to the Military (RAM) can be extended to internal control. A breakdown of respect for government will lessen the ability of state agencies to elicit, shape and contain movements within society.

Furthermore, a process of social atomization may well leave

(widespread) enthusiasms as the major way in which activists are motivated. These enthusiasts will, in some cases, be unwilling to accept the disciplines of citizenship. This will be true not only in non-democratic states, but also in their democratic counterparts. Subordination to majority opinions, and mutual tolerance against the background of the rule of law, will entail a degree of restraint that is unwelcome to many.

It is unclear that states, whatever their capacity for surveillance, will be able to contain the consequent tension or suppress the resulting violence. In part, this is due to the difficulty of the task, and, in part, a response to the constraints affecting their response. The balance of restraint will continue to move against the forces of the state, and will be enforced by legal systems that frequently have scant understanding of the problems of acting against terrorists. These difficulties will be compounded by the political willingness to buy off terrorists with amnesties, a process that encourages further violence, undermines peaceful opposition movements, and accentuates the conflation of criminality and terrorism. More seriously, such a process defies the sense of justice that is important in encouraging popular consent and also the effective operation of democratic societies.

As a consequence of the difficulty of repressing disorder, peace-keeping as a military task will interact with what has been seen as the breakdown, or at least reconceptualization, of the state. This is a concept frequently expressed by referring to the post-Westphalian state: the transition of state authority away from the monopolization of sovereignty that stemmed in Europe from the Peace of Westphalia of 1648, the sovereign state, towards a more diffuse situation in which national states wield less authority, and sovereignty is multiple.

The weakness of government will be linked in some states to the presence of insurrectionary movements. This will be particularly acute in the case of separatist movements, which affect states from the very large ones, such as India, to the far smaller ones, such as Moldova, which has a Russian-backed secessionist section called Transdniestria. Counter-insurgency warfare will pose a major challenge for militaries, whether high- or low-tech. The principal problem will be political: how to translate military presence into an agreed solution that permits a demilitarization of disputes. This is more important than any differentiation of counter-insurgency strategies in terms of weaponry.

A geographical perspective can be added to this by suggesting that the next century will see a recurrence of the position in Europe in 1550–1650. Then, during the so-called Wars of Religion, conflict was most serious and protracted in areas where there were appreciable numbers of both Catholics and Protestants, rather than, for example in Iberia or Scandinavia, where one group predominated. Thus, in the future, the breakdown of integrative patterns will make multi-ethnic and multi-religious states especially volatile, if the ethnic and religious groups maintain a strong tradition of group cohesion, and hostility to counterparts.

This is at once pessimistic and in need of qualification. As most states are far from homogenous, the implication would be that high levels of civil violence are, and will be, present. Yet, the former is not the case. Practices of prejudice and discrimination, as well as the maintenance of cohesion through endogamy, confessional education, and inheritance and employment practices, are not the same as organized violence. However, as Nigeria, Northern Ireland, Rwanda, Sri Lanka, Yugoslavia and other states showed in the late twentieth century, they retained this potential. This is likely to set the pace of civil conflict over the next century.

Religious fault-lines are particularly powerful at the edges of the Islamic world, especially in South Asia, the Balkans, and in Africa. In 2000, disputes between Christians and Muslims led to bloody riots in Kaduna in northern Nigeria, as well as to religious conflict in Indonesia's Molucca Islands in which some soldiers took a role. Also in Indonesia in 2000, there has been separatist and inter-religious violence in the Aceh region of Sumatra. In the Philippines, there is no sign of the end of the long-lasting conflict between the government and the Moro Islamic Liberation Front on Mindanao. Indeed, in 2000 the Front's leader, Hashim Salamat, called for a *jihad*.

Religious differences challenge not only the peace of both Indonesia and India but also their identity, as the secular ideology of the post-independence period is supplanted by religious-based notions of national identity, respectively Muslim and Hindu. This is an important clue to future instability that will have international as well as domestic consequences, for such shifts make it difficult to accept compromise solutions to disputes. The ability of religious groups to focus and exacerbate other tensions and to challenge the state is not restricted to Islam. In Africa, for example, it can be seen in Uganda with the Holy Spirit Movement.

As the resilience of religion, despite secularist analyses, assumptions and policies, has been one of the major themes of the last decade, it is likely that religion will remain important to the agenda and context of domestic politics, and indeed international relations, over the next century. Religious identity and antagonism help overcome restraints against violence, especially against the killing of neighbours. They also do not lend themselves to compromise. Furthermore, thanks to both proselytism and different birth rates among religious groups, confessional relations are necessarily dynamic, or, to use a different but equally appropriate phrase, unstable.

As a consequence, it is likely that religious antagonisms will play a major role in civil conflict over the next century. This is underrated by some Western commentators who are apt to identify religious antagonism with the past and particularly not with the Western world. The attitudes of Western religious leaders help support this approach as they stress ecumenical approaches. In addition, both theology and religious teaching in the West searches for common themes among religions.

Yet these approaches are not only a misleading description of the potential of religious hatred throughout the world, but may also underrate the likely role of such hatred in the West. In particular, church hierarchies and established practices may find that religious fundamentalism has a greater impact within Christianity. This fundamentalism might be directed at less ardent Christians as well as non-believers. Movements of religious renewal do not have to be benign.

The failure of many governments to monopolize weaponry, to delegitimate internal violence, and to control their own states does not have to lead to civil warfare, but it is very serious when linked to the absence or demise of consensual politics. Looked at differently, this absence or demise encourages the former. The net result is civil war of some type, although this civil warfare can be variously defined. It may be no more than the armed defiance of the state seen with powerful gangs practising 'narcoterrorism', which is a major problem in Mexico, some South American countries, especially Colombia, much of the West Indies, and several countries in South Asia. Such 'narcoterrorism' is likely to grow as the profitability of the drugs trade will remain high, and as such practices offer effective tax evasion. Alternatively, there may be some significant ethnic, religious, regional or political dimension to the struggle.

Furthermore, the two may overlap, as with the FARC and ELN guerrilla movements in Colombia, both of which use force to hold sway over drug-growing areas and profit from the trade, as the Viet Cong also did during the Vietnam War. With the 'war on drugs' policy, the American government seeks to overcome the conflation of guerrilla movements with the drugs trade, but, paradoxically, it is American demand for drugs that finances this nexus. The American state uses methods against drug producers and dealers in Latin America (and adopts a militarized stance to this end) that it is unwilling to pursue within the USA for reasons of civil liberties, but also politics.

There is no rule that protects democratic societies and

Western states from domestic challenges such as narcoterrorism. Indeed, both are increasingly affected by what can be seen as higher levels of potential instability, although this is a long way from the classic civil war. This instability can be viewed in several ways. It can be seen as an inevitable by-product of organized life, in some way integral to human society. In other words, the inability to cope with dissent short of violence should not be seen as a failure of incorporation, but rather as an inherent characteristic of social life. This would suggest the need for constant counter-practices and doctrine, not least readiness for militarized policing and for a flexible, but firm, approach to law and order.

Yet, such a functional approach might be presented as overly complacent. In particular, it can be argued that recent, and continuing, social and cultural developments are such that this 'by-product' view underrates the stresses created by violence, and also the extent to which this violence, and its threat, are growing in scale. The first point would focus on the sensitivity of modern society to disruption. This is a matter of economic activity and psychological disruption. The first, arguably, can be costed. Furthermore, this costing can be brought into the equation and can be countered by insurance. Nevertheless, current developments, in particular in Russia, but also far more widely, suggest that the interaction of criminality and business is such as to distort, if not dominate, economic patterns and to wrest surveillance and control of much of the economy from the state. Widespread fraud and tax evasion can be seen as facets of the latter.

This situation is not only true of some of the ex-Communist states seeking to create a new public culture. Rampant fraud, a lack of any sense of equity in government, and a response that appears to deny its role, also characterize a wide range of countries, including, for example Nigeria and Pakistan. The problem is sufficiently widespread to encourage a crisis of legitimacy in government, leading to periodic military takeovers, as in Brazil and Turkey, and, in turn, to disillusionment with the armed forces. In such a situation, the military, despite their pretensions to stand for national identity and to maintain order, can appear to their critics to be little different from the mercenary forces that have played a role in the politics of a number of countries in recent years, including New Guinea and Sierra Leone. Indeed, Western attitudes to the military do not pertain in many other states.

A lack of legitimacy in both civilian government and military opposition was posed in Paraguay in 2000. An unpopular civilian government under an unelected President, Luis Macchi, presiding over 16 per cent unemployment as well as widespread poverty and corruption, was faced by a military coup by supporters of a former army chief, Lino Oviedo. The coup failed when the rebels were unable to win sufficient military support, but, alongside the military coup in Ecuador in January 2000, it was a warning about the readiness to use force to remove apparently unsuccessful and discredited civilian governments.

Civil conflict can take many forms. An approach that emphasizes the destabilizing consequences of fraud, in short an illegal, but not necessarily a violent, resistance to government may seem a long way from traditional conceptions of civil war, but, instead, it serves as a reminder of the need for dynamic definitions of conflict, resistance and control.

To look ahead, another version of the same might occur in the European super-state that is on the drawing board. In order to meet its pretensions to power, and its policies of economic intervention, social welfare and regional assistance, the European Union is likely to have a high tax burden, both direct and indirect. In some, by then, formerly distinct countries, such as Britain, this will run counter to assumptions, and past practices, of low taxation. Yet, there will be no effective way to express dissent within the existing governmental or political process. This is likely to legitimate a sense of grievance and to lead to widespread tax avoidance practices.

It is easy to see how such processes will lead to violence. Governmental agencies will act as bailiffs, seizing property, and will mount intrusive surveillance operations. These will lead to violence, which could easily be widespread. Furthermore, there may well be opposition between centrally controlled European agencies and their local counterparts and rivals, most obviously between European and 'regional' police forces. Whether the net effect is widespread local violence or a full-blooded secessionist movement, the resulting situation will be difficult to contain. Thus, civil warfare can be seen as the consequence of the pretensions of state structures that do not enjoy public confidence. This is particularly the case if popularly elected local governments are to be intimidated, as with the treatment of Austria by the European Union in 2000.

This is a different approach from that which approaches violence within the West as a consequence of radical insurrectionary movements directed against the democratic state, but is a reminder that the process of presenting the state as a moral absolute, legitimated by democratic processes, is one that can be, and will be, contested from a number of directions. Leaving aside the moral absolute, the very notion of legitimation by democratic processes, whether within a state or within a superstate such as the European Union, can be challenged by anti-authoritarian discourses and practices, that deny the 'tyranny of the majority'; while, conversely, claims to the democratic character of particular processes can also be refuted.

The former point is particularly relevant given some of the prospects that can be outlined for human society. In particular, it is probable that resource issues and environmental pressures will cause acute pressures within societies. These will vary by country, but, as already discussed, there are likely to be competing demands for land, water and subsidies, and also pressures relating to environmental quality. These will probably lead to an increased emphasis on government regulation. In some contexts, such regulation is only effective if it amounts, directly or indirectly, by edict or pricing policy, to prohibition. Thus, for example, concern about energy availability and environmental damage may lead to bans on the ownership or use of motor cars, demands on housing stock to the allocation of rooms deemed spare within individual dwellings, water rationing to the prohibition of garden hoses or dishwashers or daily showers, and so on. However much defended on policy grounds and however much supported by political processes, such policies are likely to seem revolutionary, and to strike many as unfair, illegal and an abuse. The resulting challenge may have, in many states, a political and legal focus, but, in others, the threshold of acts of collective violence may be reached more rapidly.

A degree of regulation that might seem acceptable in wartime will not seem so in peace. Furthermore, the degree of regulation that was accepted, or enforced, during the two World Wars of the twentieth century, is now unacceptable, thanks in large part to the social changes of the late twentieth century. This is less true of non-Western societies in large part because of levels of repression, but also owing to different practices of social conformity.

Such a prospectus may strike some readers as overly similar to the ramblings of Montana militiamen, but it is intended to underline the extent to which anti-authoritarianism will have a broad range. In addition, it is likely to involve the state in widespread policing that may well elicit a violent response.

Furthermore, reference to the integrative characteristics of national societies and democratic political systems should not necessarily lead to the assumption that opponents are marginal. Indeed, in the case of democracies, the opponents notionally may be a narrow minority of the electorate and, indeed, a majority of the adult population, as many of the latter will not have voted. Again, this challenges concepts of legitimacy. In Britain, the absence of proportional representation ensures that highly unpopular legislation is passed by a government elected by only a minority of the electorate.

The importance of the American model has to be noted here, although traditions of violent resistance to governmental authority are present in many democratic states, for example France. Suspicion of a standing (permanent) governmental threat to rights and liberties is central to American public culture. The notion of consent as an active principle is very much present in America, as is a belief in the value of weak government. In the field of arms, suspicion of government has led to a resilient emphasis on the right to own and bear them, and to an accompanying practice of gun ownership and use, by both men and women, unprecedented elsewhere in the Western world (although there are high rates of ownership in some Latin American countries, such as Brazil). In the military sphere, traditionally there has been an emphasis in America on militia, which led to the development of the National Guard.

As an element of society capable of state-to-state violence, the personal right to bear arms and the American militia tradition are no longer of consequence. America's neighbours are no longer polities that can be threatened by armed citizenry, as when Spanish rule was challenged in West Florida and Mexican authority was overthrown in Texas. Instead, through its federal government, America developed the world's leading military in the twentieth century in order to assert and defend its international position and interests.

However, American public culture and politics ensured that there was no comparable attempt to increase the military power of the state within the USA. The federal government has developed surveillance and coercive agencies capable of using force, for example the Federal Bureau of Investigation and the Drug Enforcement Agency; but these were reactive, and are also heavily constrained by a powerful independent judicial system and by the continued power of other governmental bodies, especially at the state level, that are more responsive to popular expectations.

Looking ahead, it is difficult to see this situation changing, whatever the challenge. Terrorist actions in which large numbers of Americans were killed (the Oklahoma Bombing of 1997) or could have been killed (the World Trade Center Bombing), did not lead to a drive to change the nature of internal policing. The federal government has created teams to counter the threat of chemical and biological terrorism, and there have been improvements in surveillance, but, in practical terms, the emphasis will remain on reaction to crises of disorder and law-lessness, rather than on pro-active measures likely to lessen their risk. The latter would be rejected as authoritarian and would, indeed, probably trigger crises.

The influence of this American model is noted elsewhere through the impact of the media. Much of this, especially cinema and television, is dominated by production for the American market, the most affluent in the world, and therefore has to make sense in terms of its suppositions. However, the exportability of the American model in terms of state practice is far less clear. Whereas American economic policies will continue to be exported, and will retain the aura of American prosperity and economic growth, it is far less clear that this will be the case in other respects. This is true not only of American gun culture, but also of dominant American attitudes to the rela-tionship between individual and group provision of social welfare and personal rights, and thus of the notion of a legal restriction on state powers and state-directed change expressed through the constitution.

To turn further afield, it is unclear whether the model of capitalist economic growth, state regulation, governmental pro-vision of social welfare, and centralized definition and control of individual rights, the practice in most of the Western world outside the USA, will continue to be viable. If it does not continue to be viable, this is likely to be profoundly disorientat-ing for individuals and groups, and this disorientation is likely to lead to violence both against governmental agencies and structures, and against others seen as benefiting from change or threatening traditional practices, for example immigrant labour. In short, a collapse of the viability of the state may well lead to an eruption of violence, while attempts to enhance this viability may also lead to resistance.

In the 1930s, the crisis of the capitalist model helped produce a new authoritarianism in the shape of Nazi Germany and other states characterized by populism, corporatism and autarky; and this was followed by World War II. At present, this seems less likely, if only because state structures and myths are weaker and social discipline less pronounced. It is unclear whether the situation will be altered by another major economic downturn. Widespread unemployment, linked to globalist pressures, led, in the early 1980s and again in the early 1990s, to the panacea of social welfare, rather than to authoritarian governments and governmental direction of national resources.

However, economic difficulties can also be associated with the rise of far-right political parties, for example in modern Austria, France and Germany. These parties adopted an adversarial language, analysis and platform defining, and focusing on, enemies within and abroad, especially immigrants. Such policies were a threat to civic peace, and were one of these parties to gain control of a major state then it is likely that its policies would be confrontational.

The most likely scenario would be in post-Communist Russia. Much of the discussion about Russia as a future military power focuses on the damage done to its military capability by the disruption attendant on, and subsequent to, the fall of the Soviet system. The conclusion drawn is that Russia is no longer able to challenge the West, and attention has accordingly switched both to China and to 'rogue states'. This may be true at present, but two caveats may be offered. First, defeated or 'failed' powers have had an ability to recover rapidly, for example Rome during the Second Punic War, England in the 1650s, Britain after 1783, France in 1792–94, and Germany after

1918. It can be argued that the role of resources and technology has removed any such potential in the modern world, and/or that the depths of Russia's decline tend to the same conclusion. However, over the timespan of a century, this account is less clear. This is particularly so given the potential for paradigm shifts in military history (whether or not they are presented as revolutions in military history).

Secondly, even if Russia may not be seen as potent (in relative terms) as it was at the height of the Cold War, it may soon be more potent in absolute terms, and, irrespective of this, retains the capacity to take an aggressive stance towards its neighbours. Thus, the potential for fascistic and populist tendencies within Russia is troubling, and this cannot be greatly lessened by reference to its military weakness. The situation is especially troubling in the Caucasus region and Central Asia, because they are also inherently unstable, while Russian power also remains a potential element in any Balkan crisis.

To return to the Western world as a whole, the widespread decline in senses of nationhood and communitarianism will ensure that, in depressions, the 'haves', whether affluent or at least defined as such through retaining their jobs, do not identify with those who are less successful. This will encourage the growth of the so-called 'underclass'. In addition, the entry into it of those formerly with jobs may lead to a higher rate of militancy.

The 'underclass' can respond to adverse circumstances in a number of ways. Most will try to enter or re-enter productive employment, but, for many, this can take the form of illegal behaviour or of behaviour judged anti-social, for example prostitution. Others will be encouraged to reject existing norms and institutions in a more organized fashion. This is likely to become increasingly the case because higher rates of educational access will allow more people to express their sense of alienation in a more coherent fashion. Whereas the student revolts of the 1960s were primarily by middle-class children expressing outrage, not suffering, those in the following century will probably be of students and ex-students demanding action because their prospects do not live up to their expectations.

Alongside this socio-economic crisis, there will be a rejection of dominant values that reflects an alienation in which boredom and the desire for change, especially intoxicating change, will play a large role. This alienation can be seen in a positive light, as a response to the potentially stultifying grip of former generations, but there can also be a destructive aspect. This can take the form of revolutionary enthusiasms that contribute to a cycle of violence. Looking to the future, it is possible that, in reaction to socio-economic tensions, nihilism will have an appeal to many. This is a dangerous prospect, because, if on any great scale, it threatens social stability.

Social mobility is seen by most as a one-way street and one in which there is a demand for instant gratification, rather than a long-term process to which the individual has to contribute greatly. The notion of social mobility through education and opportunity for all is a response to economic changes in which the emphasis is on a skilled workforce. This is then seen as a counterpart to a democratic civic politics. Yet, it is just as likely that fluid labour markets and economic demands will produce a situation in which the few have skills and services that are highly regarded and well rewarded, while the many have nothing in particular to offer and will find their wage rates eroded by global competition, and, within their own countries, by machinization and other processes. In short, globalism, its processes and problems, will be internalized with destructive consequences.

It is unclear whether this social-economic model will corrode civic politics. The few may well reject expropriatory taxation, and flee the jurisdiction of high-taxing states, but, more seriously, the many may well be unable to accept the consequences of downward social mobility and economic returns, especially as their expectations will have been very different. There will be a sense of alienation by job-holders and citizens that will pose serious problems for political systems; as well, probably, as leading to protectionism, violence towards immigrants, and other aspects of domestic and international tension.

The great engine of economic growth that powered Western prosperity and democratic politics after 1945 may not go on having such benign effects as it has hitherto. In addition, aside from theoretical points about the cyclical character of economic growth, there are also practical points about the impact of demographic growth, and thus falling per capita benefits, as well as about the impact of resource shortages and of competition from non-Western growth.

It will be the case that if growth is linked to democracy, and both to peacefulness, in international relations and domestic politics, then this diffusion of economic expansion outside the West should not be a threat, an interpretation that is actively pressed by supporters of free trade. However, it is not clear that this benign model will describe the strains within Western societies over the next century. These strains may contribute to a damaging impression of uncertainty and decline which will be potent whatever the experience of the average individual.

Anyway, in a democratized society, aggregate growth rates are less important than the per capita impact, as well as the numbers affected by downward movements. As already suggested, the latter is likely to be under pressure from population growth, especially if problems of resource availability increase the real cost of resource extraction and use faster than the rate of improvements in utilization. Put crudely, and the following is subject to qualification, economic growth will occur, and at a high rate in some spheres, but not at an overall rate capable of assuaging socio-economic demands, fears and expectations. The consequences will impact on weak governmental structures, on systems of public politics that are not attuned to long-term crises of this nature, and on societies where support for modernization, or, at least, for many of its consequences, is limited while opposition is often bitter. The result will be a search for governmental, collective and individual solutions that exacerbates insecurity and provides issues and occasions for violence.

3 War and the International Order: the Future

> Deterrence never was, and cannot ever be, construed as an appropriate response to every military threat.
>
> Pascal Boniface, 'France and the dubious charms of a post-nuclear world', in David Haglund (ed.), *Pondering NATO's Nuclear Options: Gambits for a Post-Westphalian World* (1999)

With this chapter, we return to a more conventional account of warfare. To most readers, wars are fought between armies (and navies and air forces), and these are the forces of states. In this chapter, I will look at the likely cause of future wars, and in the next I will turn to how they will be fought. These are not simply matters of speculation, but are actively debated and planned by the military. It would be inappropriate for scholars to be restricted to such analyses, not least because the experience of the past suggests that most wars do not conform to war plans, and the same is of course true of battles, campaigns and the use of particular weapons. Nevertheless, attention to such planning is a reminder that the purpose of military capability is as much future contingency as present task.

Looking to the future, it is possible to seek general causes of dispute, specific disputes between individual states, and the absence of an effective system of adjudication. The first, in part, relate to the resource issues discussed in the last chapter. Rising global demands will be played out in a world in which the availability of resources and population pressures both vary greatly. Although the most sensible ways to maintain and enhance resources require international co-operation, it is likely that confrontation and conflict will arise from unilateral attempts to redistribute resources. The situation is likely to be particularly acute with resources that can flow or move across borders, for example water, oil and fish.

The limited supply and, in places, near-exhaustion of such resources will pose a major problem. Already-acute disputes over control of, and access to, the water, in the systems of the Ganges, Tigris, Euphrates and Jordan will become more serious and will be joined by other river systems. Some tensions, for example between Canada and the USA, or, more specifically, British Columbia and California, and between Mexico and Texas, and, perhaps, between Kazakhstan and Uzbekistan over the Aral Sea, will be contained peacefully, but they will still engender stress; other disputes will entail violence.

For example, it is difficult to be optimistic about the situation on the West Bank of the Jordan where water is both in short supply and unequally distributed between Palestinians and Israeli settlers. The latter use about five times as much per person as the former, in part because of extensive irrigation. Many Palestinians lack piped water. An optimistic solution would envisage more provision, by desalination, and less use, by changing farming practices; but a pessimist would anticipate no such scenario and would instead predict conflict over surface water and aquifers. In addition, around much of the world, the offshore availability of oil and fish will ensure that disputes over borders and territorial waters, for example in the South China Sea and the Persian Gulf, will become more serious.

Concern over resources has accentuated interest in boundaries. The pressures of growth, the intensification of regional economies, and the globalization of the world economy will continue to lead to a situation in which the search for, and utilization of, resources become ever more widespread and important. This will be exacerbated by the exhaustion of established resources, and the possibilities of profitable exploitation in regions hitherto deemed inaccessible or unprofitable.

This will enforce the division of the world surface, on both land and sea, for exploration, and production companies have to know from which state they should acquire rights. Thus the intensification of frontier disputes will be a consequence of rising economic demand. Furthermore, the possibility that resources may be discovered will continue to encourage territorial disputes, any of which may become violent or precipitate other tensions. For example, in 1995, Romania and Ukraine contested the possession of Serpent Island off the Romanian coast as part of a discussion designed to prepare for a treaty between the two states. The Romanian Foreign Minister told the Senate that, although the island was not then an asset, it might become one, owing to oil and natural gas reserves. Under the 1982 United Nations Convention on the Law of the Sea, islands, as well as mainland possessions, have to be taken into account in defining maritime zones. Islands such as the Hawar Islands, contested by force between Bahrain and Qatar in the 1980s, and the Red Sea islands, fought over between Eritrea and Yemen in 1995, have become contentious as a result of the actual or possible prospect of oil. In 2000, a dispute between Guyana and Surinam over offshore oil concessions became violent.

More generally, defence, aggrandizement and security will focus on preserving, expanding and protecting access to resources, as states struggle to meet the needs of their populations and to defend their places in the global economic system. The 1999 Global Environment Outlook report, *GEO 2000*, produced by the United Nations Environment Programme, predicted environmental degradation and population growth, leading to the possibility, in the first quarter of the current century, of 'water wars' over scarce resources in North Africa and South-West Asia. Interest in mineral resources has helped encourage and sustain the intervention of Angola, Namibia, Rwanda, Uganda and Zimbabwe in Congo, and there is every sign that this will continue: the diamonds and gold that can be gained are readily negotiable. Similarly, Liberia has backed the rebel RUF in Sierra Leone, in part in order to gain control of diamond deposits.

International conflict over resources may also involve attempts to redistribute wealth at a global level, and, as such, will be a new version of the wars launched by revisionist powers (those seeking to change the status quo). This attempted redistribution does not have to take the form of military conflict, but the language of combat is, and will be, employed, with reference to global economic relations, and more specifically, to trade wars or blockades. The concept of exploitation, and resistance to it, is presented in terms of conflict.

Aside from raising the question of how best to define war, this issue serves as a reminder that the economic globalization which is seen by some as a safeguard of peace through interdependency is also unpopular, resisted and subject to serious internal strains. The high rates of volatility and interdependency in the global economy are such that trade wars and fiscal restrictions will indeed be able to do an enormous amount of harm, and quickly.

They may indeed be seen as the most effective form of warfare for major states, although interdependency means precisely that. For example, trade or investment bans may harm civilians not responsible for government policy in the country thus blockaded, as well as harming exporting industries in the blockading country. Banning imports may encourage domestic production, but, if that is more expensive, it can also lead to inefficiencies, as well as encouraging a pattern of state intervention in the economy that is inherently inefficient. The extent to which solvency and credit are the product of a confidence that can be rapidly damaged by hostile international actions suggests that traditional forms of trade wars, that focus on the prohibition of the movement and/or consumption of goods, may be less effective than those that focus directly on the availability and value of money and financial instruments, especially credit instruments. Wall Street and the IMF can have far more influence than warships offshore. This is particularly so given the declining role of manufacturing industry in employment and economic activity, certainly as far as many Western countries are concerned.

To discuss the future of war in such terms may appear strange but, in fact, it is a reminder of the degree to which war is not simply about fighting, as well as underlining the fact that international tensions can be between allies and other states that may wish to pursue hostile acts without risking the commitments of military conflict. As suggested elsewhere in this study, however, it is necessary to note the diversity of warfare. A futuristic vision of conflict focusing on exchange rates and liquidity may be appropriate in the event of clashes between, say, the USA, Japan and the European Union, or may be used by the last to discipline Britain, and other recalcitrant members; but such an assessment appears far less appropriate for state-to-state relations between less economically developed states, let alone for civil conflict.

What is unclear is how far economic warfare will be used against 'rogue' states, and with what success. The current crop of such states uses self-sufficiency, brutal domestic control, and, in some cases, for example Libya, oil wealth, to restrict the effectiveness of such warfare. It is unclear whether the same will be true of future 'rogue' states.

Furthermore, there is the issue of timing. Financial and commercial retribution could be very rapid, but may not have a sufficiently rapid impact to change the attitude of autarchic regimes. They will be able to pass on the costs to their subjects, and to use these in order to rally domestic support for the regime. This underlines the question of how best to take action against states, an issue in which legality, pragmatism and capability interact. At present, there are attempts to place clear legal restraints on military and other actions, but it could be argued that their effectiveness depends on the state in question that proposes action. This is true of its domestic political culture as well as its international strength. The role of an independent judiciary, legitimated adversarial politics, free press and articulate public opinion in states such as the USA and Britain ensures that international restraints will probably continue to have a powerful domestic echo. This is far less clear for many other states.

Resource tensions in the future will interact with already existing disputes, for example over borders, as well as creating new ones. To turn to specifics, while it is likely that water and oil will be the foci of conflict, there will also be serious disputes over both the general terms of trade and their impact on pricing and availability. Import restrictions will be presented as exporting unemployment, leading to demands for retribution. Transport and access will also remain an issue, especially for landlocked states, such as Ethiopia and Nepal, and may become more so as resource issues become more pressing and trade becomes more important in particular economies. Indeed, disputes over transit through Eritrea helped to cause its conflict with Ethiopia at the close of the 1990s.

Globalism and greater interdependency will exacerbate as much as lessen tensions. For example, greater prosperity, combined with population growth, will help increase Chinese and Indian dependence on imports, for example of oil, and thus their sensitivity to the availability and distribution of resources. It is unclear whether the two powers will learn how to operate, balance and advance their interests within the international community, as powers seeking a long-term and stable position must, or whether they will strive for advantage in a fashion that elicits opposing actions and, possibly, war. In short, the nature and objectives of regional hegemony, and its relationship with the global situation, can vary greatly.

This is particularly a problem as far as the near-neighbours of regional powers are concerned. One of the major risks of conflict at present, and in the foreseeable future, arises from challenges to the notion of regional hegemony. These challenges come from two sources: first, local opposition and, second, the notion of a liberal universalism which, to its critics, is a cover for Western, more particularly American, hegemony. Thus, powerful states, such as China, India and Russia, expect to dominate their neighbours and do not appreciate opposition. This practice is made more dangerous by the relationship between regional hegemony and control over frontier areas. Thus, for example, each of the major powers cited has serious problems with opposition in frontier areas – especially in Kashmir for India, the northern Caucasus for Russia, and Tibet and Xinjiang for China – and these problems are likely to continue. Furthermore, both military intervention and political dynamics have made it difficult for these powers to compromise or back down, further ensuring the intractability of the situation. This difficulty ensures that it will often be impossible to adopt or sustain an attitude towards 'hegemony' or 'control' that does not alienate other powers. Thus, the notion of buffer zones, and the equivalent in terms of attitudes, is not developed, or is only poorly developed.

For China, the principal military challenges in the future may come not from Western powers, but, rather, as in the long centuries down to the 1830s, from within China and along its land borders. For example, separatism in Xinjiang may interact with and encourage Chinese intervention in the Central Asian republics. Islamic links, real or feared, between domestic and international opponents of China, may encourage such intervention. Alternatively, China may be drawn into conflict between Vietnam and its neighbours, as in 1979, or between India and Pakistan, or into Burma. The extent to which such conflict triggers confrontation with the West (and/or Russia) will depend on the degree of flexibility that these powers, especially the USA, show. That will be very difficult, not least because of the pressures of liberal globalism and the notion of geopolitical linkages, and because compromise is not a virtue in the public politics of different societies.

At a lesser scale, other would-be local hegemons include Turkey, Syria, Iraq, Iran, Pakistan, Brazil, South Africa and Nigeria. Each has reasons to seek to dominate at least one neighbouring state, and, for each, such dominance is a matter of more than simply 'realist' calculation of geopolitical need. Instead, strategic cultures (notions about the alleged inherent relationship between national identity and regional hegemony), that reflect ideas and attitudes spread and encouraged by governing élites, play a role, as does the drive to appear populist that affects even (and often especially) the most dictatorial of regimes.

Furthermore, the instability of regions such as the Caucasus, Central Asia, Afghanistan and Lebanon will encourage intervention, in order both to cement and to overthrow particular situations. As with the relationship between civil conflict and the absence or weakness of democracy, there will be a lack of a strong alternative to force in order to legitimate and sustain desirable outcomes. The interaction of hegemony and neighbouring weakness will continue, and will help to sustain instability. Aside from regions already mentioned, it is necessary to include Central Africa and the Sudan, and, looking ahead, probably Burma and Indonesia. As in Central Africa, the resulting chaos will not observe state frontiers, and the resulting export of violence will encourage intervention. Thus, India, China and Thailand may intervene in some fashion in Burma.

The USA does not face challenges on this scale. There are questions about the long-term stability of Canada and Mexico, but these are different in type. Nevertheless, concern helped motivate American support for NAFTA (North American Free Trade Area). This offers a form of stabilization that is different from military interventionism of the type of Syria in Lebanon. It is, and will be, very difficult for Americans to understand the degree to which a number of regional hegemons feel it necessary to overawe their neighbours, in part in order to maintain internal order and also control over frontier regions.

This overawing will reflect an entirely different concept of stability and legitimacy to those of modern liberal Western opinion. The traditional basis of international stability, namely the mutual respect of sovereignty, and the accustomed practices, of regional hegemony and balance of power politics, have been eroded, or at least challenged, by the claims of globalist politics based on international standards of rulership, and on the panoptic eye, or at least lens, of the media. However, this traditional basis was also largely a Western view, in that the mutual respect of sovereignty was a concept that has less meaning in, for example, Chinese and Islamic thought. Furthermore, although Western concepts were spread during the age of imperialism, and in the period of decolonization, and were expressed in a myriad of treaties, alternatives have retained a certain potency. Nevertheless, the current thesis of most governments is based on an integrity that is expressed in terms of sovereignty. This is challenged by external attempts to prescribe rules.

Liberal internationalism is likely to cause conflict unless it is restrained by a prudential respect for traditional power politics. This will be a difficult balance to strike, not least as the task will fall on American leaders who are neither best prepared for it, nor able to play to a domestic constituency that understands international power politics and the validity of alternative value systems. Standing up for America strikes a chord with American public opinion, but other states standing up for themselves, especially if in different terms, do not win American understanding, with the exception of Israel which is seen by an influential section of American opinion as almost an extension of America. In addition, American attitudes will be affected by a determination to see as normal an economic world that enables the USA to use its investment capital, operational control and purchasing power to gain a very disproportionate share in per capita terms of global resources

In 1990, the Gulf War brought a happy convergence of Western resource interests and a ready response to a clear-cut aggression by an unpopular non-Western power that made it relatively easy to sustain widespread support for action. Such a convergence is unlikely to recur in this fashion.

It will remain unclear whether internationalism is based on a sensible assessment of means and goals. On one level, such an assessment will depend on the restraint displayed by the cartography of Western concern. Will there be a war to drive China from Tibet, or military intervention to try to resolve conflicts in the Caucasus or Central Africa? It is likely that the reality of a new world order will be more restrained than the language; but that can suggest a misleading complacency. In particular, the notion of a clear or static boundary defining a zone where it is safe to intervene is questionable. So, also, is the notion that other states will readily be able to distinguish a language of global order from the practice of a more limited pattern of commitment. Wars frequently arise as the product of the interaction of bellicosity and what could be regarded as a misjudgement of the resolve of other powers, and there is no reason to believe that this situation will alter. Distrust is a constant factor, as is the multitude of reasons for powers misunderstanding others.

Liberal internationalism will also encounter the problem that the major Western power, the USA, will continue to seek to be a global hegemon, rather than an internationalist power. The USA will continue to have an ambivalent relationship with the constraints of collective security, especially with the United Nations. It is particularly unhappy with the notion of United Nations direction of operations involving American forces, is unhappy with the possibility of United Nations controls over policy towards, say, Israel or Cuba, and, more generally, is unwilling to accept the subordination of American jurisdictions and interests to their international counterparts. By mid-2000, the USA was close to $2 billion in arrears on its United Nations dues.

These positions are not without point. To take the first, it is far from clear that United Nations military structures are adequate. There are particular problems with United Nations staff organization and practices. The use of the United Nations presupposes acceptance of the legitimacy of sovereign governments. While this may be the case in international law, it is easy to appreciate why Americans (and others), who live in democratic societies and have democratically elected governments, will continue to oppose giving authority to the representatives of undemocratic societies and autocratic regimes. Both are well represented in the United Nations, which, despite its aspirations, reflects the lack of any homogeneity of culture and values in the world. To turn to the future, it is also easy to predict a rift between international bodies using egalitarian arguments to demand the redistribution of resources and Western societies resisting such processes. This will undermine the United Nations.

Furthermore, aside from their difficulties with the United Nations, American politicians and public opinion will continue instinctively to think in unilateral, not multilateral, terms. There will continue to be tensions between the external constraints that alliance policy-making entails and the nature of political culture in the USA, which tends to be hostile to compromise with foreign powers and also to not trust them to observe their commitments. The notion of American exceptionalism does not encourage the exigencies of compromise, while the history of American foreign policy is that of American leadership, and thus does not lead to an interpretation of alliances as based on mutual needs. American politicians argue that Congress can supersede treaty obligations.

It is unclear how far American politicians will remain convinced of the value of long-standing commitments, for example in Europe. The history of American engagement in Africa suggests that it is entirely possible to follow a spasmodic course, dictated by immediate concerns, and, more generally, by neglect. Except for the alliance structure provided by NATO (North Atlantic Treaty Organization), it is possible that that would also be the pattern in a post-Cold War Europe. Conversely, American concerns about China might lead future American governments to seek European and Russian support. What is less clear is how they will choose if it is not possible to have both.

For the Americans, European enlargement is a goal as it can lead to the 'anchoring' of strategically important states, particularly Turkey and even Russia, in the Western camp. However, this process may not work from the American perspective. A stronger Europe may be neutralist, forcing the Americans to look elsewhere for allies. This is likely to be particularly the case if Russia plays a role in European security structures. This may well lead to the neutralization of NATO. Conversely, a future Europe may exclude, and be in rivalry with, Russia, giving America a choice of allies against China, or the European Union may fail, leading to a situation in which 'Europe' involves a variety of options and problems for the USA.

It is not inevitable that an expansionist and/or aggressive China will turn against Russia. In World War II, despite its Manchurian empire and ideological hostility to Communism, Japan turned against the USA, not the Soviet Union. Nevertheless, a Russia determined to retain its position in the Far East, needing to secure its Siberian resources, and wary of Chinese–Islamic links, is likely to see China as hostile. On geostrategic lines, this should encourage Russian co-operation with the USA, but such a relationship can easily be mishandled in an atmosphere of distrust and as a result of the search for national interest. Concern over American globalist pretensions and particular policies may lead to an identification of the USA as a threat that encourages a positive Russian response to Chinese approaches. Furthermore, in an echo of the dispute over responsibility for the appeasement of Nazi Germany by the Western powers and the Soviet Union, a less than robust American response to Chinese intimidation of Taiwan may lead the Russians to feel that America cannot be trusted. Concern about the position in the Russian Far East may also lead to a sense that it would be better for Russia if China and the USA fought.

All of these factors will create problems for American governments. They will accentuate the habitual American distrust of allies and lend new force to it, because, hitherto, the

Americans have not had to anchor their foreign policy on co-operation with a state and society deemed hostile. Yet, it is unlikely that America will wish to confront China without at least a powerful ally or allies.

The Americans will certainly face difficulties if this ally is Russia. For a number of reasons, it is unlikely that Russia will make a rapid recovery from its current problems. The demographic situation will remain harsh, affecting the numbers in healthy, productive employment, and there will continue to be major difficulties in obtaining financial stabilization and economic growth. The development of close relations between criminal groups, politics and business is a threat to Russian stability and, in particular, the ability of the government to gain a sufficient tax take is likely to remain uncertain. This will challenge attempts to use resources to any planned end. As far as Russian geo-strategy is concerned, it is likely that Russian governments will find it difficult to sustain military preparedness, let alone capability enhancement, despite the hopes of their generals.

Furthermore, Russia will remain challenged by the situation in Central Asia and the Caucasus, ensuring that it has a less benign strategic situation nearby than the USA, whatever happens in the latter case in Mexico or Quebec. The problem will be compounded by Russian assertiveness, and by the possibility that such assertiveness will win domestic political support, as with President Putin's war with Chechnya in 2000.

The problems facing Russia will not prevent American consideration of using it against an aggressive China, as the two states have a long frontier and Russia retains a significant military capability, but these problems will prompt stronger interest in alternative allies. The most obvious are India and Japan. Both are major military powers, and each feels challenged by another state that is unpredictable and that may be supported by China: Pakistan and North Korea respectively. Furthermore, the Japanese economy will probably remain well integrated with that of the USA, and that of India will become more so, as the state socialism of the past is abandoned.

Yet, neither India nor Japan are comfortable in the role of allies against China. Both feel vulnerable, and correctly so, and neither wishes to lose the degree of flexibility about policy that they currently possess. In addition, their force structures and doctrines are not designed for an offensive war against China. If, in the event of war between China and the USA, India and Japan simply protect their space against Chinese attack, that will be of only limited value to the Americans. The failure of the much subsidized Pakistani and Turkish militaries to come to the support of the USA in the Gulf War of 1990–91 is a warning about any reliance on India and Japan. For political reasons, they are unlikely to take part in operations against China. Furthermore, in the event of such a war, the Indian military is likely to be most concerned about Pakistan.

Other allies will probably be found wanting in any clash with China. States as varied as Australia, Israel and Germany will not meet the requirements of American policy. Past examples, such as the Vietnam and Gulf Wars, reveal a conditionality in support that is unwelcome to America, while, on the other hand, allies feel a lack of consultation and a concern about American policy-making processes.

Concern about consultation is understandable in political terms, but poses difficulties for military planning in both the pre-conflict and conflict stages of any confrontation or war. Both pre-conflict and conflict are now very high tempo. Alliance co-operation raises issues of security as well as speed. This was seen in the Kosovo War of 1999.

Yet, the consequence of democratization is a demand for accountability in government that makes it difficult for states to accept the leadership of another or, indeed, the consequences of membership in an alliance. The notion that the latter may lead to unwelcome steps is antipathetical to the democratizing principles and practices already referred to. This reflects the extent to which nationhood does not act as a building block for global co-operation, but rather both as a delimitation of concern and a demand for independence. This is likely to be a central issue over this century and one that will provide a background to military operations. Nationhood in many cases will also be an expression of atavistic tendencies. This will not preclude alliance politics, but will condition their character.

Aside from this general point, there will also be particular tensions and dynamics within the American-led West. American leadership will act to contain the ambitions of other powers. In Europe, there is a particular problem with Germany, the most populous and economically powerful state. At present, German public culture is resolutely against territorial expansionism, but that is not the same as abandoning the desire to use national strength to secure and advance interests. This was shown clearly after the collapse of Yugoslavia when Chancellor Kohl's support for Croatia, despite its rule over Serb-inhabited areas and the anti-democratic nature of Croatia's government, helped to precipitate the crisis.

Looking to the future, the area to the east and, in particular, south-east of Germany appears, at least in part, unstable. Taking the notion that power abhors a vacuum, and that it is difficult to contain problems, it is possible to suggest that German politicians will both want, and feel it necessary, to take the lead. Irrespective of their intentions, this may provoke local opposition and the hostility or fears of other states, particularly Russia. This concern will lead some to see American power as a guarantee, and potential curb, of German intentions.

More generally, globalism and world-wide commitments will continue to pose major problems of prioritization for the West. These may encourage restraint or, alternatively, a resort to war in order to try to settle an issue. The multiplicity of problems and commitments facing Western powers will limit the ability to respond to fresh problems. The consequent reliance on a rapid response in a particular crisis – the use of force in order to end the need to use force – will prove as unsuccessful in the future as it has often done in the past.

This reliance will also reflect the 'high-tech' nature of militaries that are designed for a very forceful response. For example, the Russian military will continue to show a preference for firepower, and, more generally, the dominance in doctrine and practice of Cold War concepts and training, rather than those possibly better attuned for low-intensity and counter-insurgency warfare. The Americans will continue to have a similar emphasis on force and response doctrines and tactics, as well as on firepower. While designed to minimize the exposure of ground troops to risk, such doctrine and tactics offer little of the alternative of militarized neighbourhood policing, with its stress on co-operation with local communities. However, in many contexts, it is the latter that is required.

Irrespective of the military means, long-range, as well as universalist, conceptions of American interests will interact with the global pretensions of the United Nations, and the sense that the settlement of international problems is a responsibility for neighbouring and other powers. The resulting premium on order, of a certain type, will encourage concern in, and about, distant areas and, conversely, insecurity in these areas about the prospect of outside interventionism. This order will also be difficult to enforce. Thus, one consequence of globalization, the wider implications of local struggles, will continue to be seriously destabilizing.

Concern about distant areas, however, will not simply reflect universalist aspirations. Instead, both military and political pressures will encourage concern and confrontation with, and even intervention in, other states, including those at a considerable range. To that extent, technology has transformed geo-politics, and, thus, military goals, capability, preparation and planning. The range of readily available modern weaponry is such that it is difficult to ignore hostile developments elsewhere, specifically the production of weapons of mass-destruction. Near-America ceases to be Cuba, which is, indeed near, and becomes North Korea; Rome can be attacked from Baghdad as well as Benghazi. The pace of change in this field will continue to be rapid, not least because it is essentially a case of the diffusion of tested technology, rather than the invention of 'super' weapons. As a result, concern will increase, as will demands for action.

Indeed, it is possible that one of the most important developments in forthcoming decades will not be the use of new military technologies (which tend to dominate the futurology of war), but the spread of established technologies to states that had not hitherto possessed them. Thus, for example, second- or third-rank powers, and also non-state movements, might be tempted to use nuclear, chemical and bacteriological weapons of mass destruction, not least because they are not inhibited by the destructiveness of such weaponry, which is also relatively inexpensive. The nature of international asymmetrical warfare, therefore, may become much more threatening to the more 'advanced' power; and its home base may be subject to attack. In turn, this vulnerability will help to drive investment in new technology, just as it will encourage the maintenance and upgrading of a strategic nuclear arsenal and the relevant delivery and control systems by the USA and, possibly, by other powers, although such a policy is expensive.

The extent to which the spread of nuclear, chemical and bacteriological weaponry will encourage the prophylactic use of force – wars, or at least the use of force, to stop the deployment of weapons systems – is unclear. Using American-supplied aircraft, the Israelis bombed the Iraqi nuclear plant at Osirak in 1981, claiming that the Iraqis were manufacturing nuclear weapons; but there has been no comparable use of force since. India and Pakistan responded to the development of nuclear weaponry by the other by stepping up their own production, rather than by launching pre-emptive strikes. The Israelis have threatened such strikes against Arab powers and Iran, but their vulnerability may, instead, encourage caution, and the Americans are very unlikely to countenance the use of planes they have supplied for such purposes. Similarly, the Americans and the Europeans have chosen to respond to the development of long-range weaponry by North Korea and Libya by defensive schemes and attempts to restrict the flow of technology, rather than by offensive action.

It is likely that this policy will continue, but it does face serious problems. These include the nature of the defensive technology, which is untested in war and reliant on very high degrees of accuracy, with scant room for error. In particular, anti-missile weaponry systems can be confused by decoys, which are of growing sophistication. Furthermore, there is the risk of exposing states to blackmail by governments that are regarded as unpredictable and unlikely to be restrained by the prospect of 'Mutually Assured Destruction'. The 'Would we have fought Hitler had he had the bomb?' question invites the response 'What alternative was there?'; but this may encourage pre-emptive strikes in the future, both by states that feel unsure of their position, and by the USA in its position as leader of Western universalism. American weakness when/if it occurs may, for example, lead a fearful Israel to launch pre-emptive attacks.

Whether or not opposing states are armed with weapons of mass-destruction, the problem of eliciting consent to their views and their conceptions of internal order will continue to face both America and the United Nations. Both will also face the problems of enforcing a verdict and, more generally, of the wasting quality of international order, in other words of the inherent fragility of such order in the face of changes and demands. The international order will require consent for its maintenance, rather than force. Force in the absence of consent may work for blasting aliens, but it is of limited value when dealing with humans. This is not intended as an anti-war remark, because the nature of communities and international systems is such that it will not be possible to rely on consent alone.

To move to the opposite position and assume that, in the future, force can operate without an attempt to build up consent, is of limited value. Indeed, the experience of the last 150 years suggests that those brought low by force have an ability to reverse the verdict, either peacefully or by violence. The high cost, political, economic and financial, both of future war and of the far more lengthy process of post-war peace maintenance, will be such that a verdict that has to be maintained by the periodic use of force will seem unacceptable to most states and societies. However, this might encourage authoritarian and intolerant states to resort to harsh domestic and international tactics, such as 'ethnic cleansing' and the encouragement of instability in neighbouring and revisionist states.

In the recent past, the most successful way to avoid the future unpicking of the verdict of war was the attempt to rebuild a civil society to which authority could be entrusted. This was seen in the treatment of West Germany, Japan and Austria after World War II, and, more generally, in the American attempt to stabilize Europe through the Marshall Plan. However, such social-political engineering was far less successful when attempted by the Americans in South Vietnam, the Soviet Union in Afghanistan, and the Israelis in Lebanon. This suggests that such policies work best when there is at least a degree of commonality in socio-economic and politico-ideological circumstances. Furthermore, the policy pursued in Germany, Japan and Austria required a total victory, and also entailed a massive post-war commitment by the victors, including occupation by conscript armies.

In the future, it is far from clear that such political costs from war and post-war are bearable; they will also exceed the available military resources of even the most powerful state. The alternative will be negotiated settlements, not total victory. Such a victory is far less typical as an attainable objective than the rhetoric of politicians, the experience of World War II or the accounts of science fiction might suggest, and this is likely to remain the case. Most wars will continue to end in negotiated settlements, not capitulations.

Yet it is unclear how future war will lead to such peaces. To do so, it will be best to wage a war in which the opposing society and government is not demonized, but that will be difficult given the need to offer a public justification for conflict, and given the unwillingness of much of the public to accept anything less than the Holocaust justification: Serbs are like Nazis and therefore we must act, the argument pursued by the West in the Kosovo crisis of 1999, and one that underrated the complexities of the situation, and represented a worrying inability to learn from the earlier Bosnian conflict when the Croats pursued 'ethnic cleansing' with as much zeal as the Serbs.

This demonization will make it difficult to negotiate peace. In the conflicts between Western powers and both Iraq and Serbia in the 1990s, the lack of an adequate exit strategy from the war became a serious cause of post-conflict political problems, and thus led to a continued need for military deployment. It is likely that similar problems will affect future Western interventions. There will certainly be no international agency capable of offering an effective system of adjudication, nor a global army that would lessen some of the current problems of internationalism. The divergence in views towards, first, the objectives of government, second, the nature and value of human rights, and, third, the use of force among the member states, will continue to be a challenge to the operation of United Nations forces and to the ability to agree goals.

For a long time, these problems were in part masked by Cold War divisions, but it is now clear that they are of a more lasting character than the struggle between Communism and the 'Free World'. After 1945, it had been hoped that the United Nations would dispose of standing forces. The Military Staff Committee that advised the Security Council sought to agree the allocation of units from the five permanent members of the Security Council, but they were unable to agree and abandoned the task in 1948. As a consequence, the United Nations developed a system that is very likely to continue in the future, a resort to *ad hoc* forces for its operations. Such combinations of the 'willing' have also been the pattern for armed actions by other collective security systems, for example by Comecon (the economic association of Communist countries) powers in Czeckoslovakia in 1967 and by NATO powers in the former Yugoslavia in the 1990s.

More generally, aspirations towards global co-operation fell victim to the central role of individual states, the reality of the Cold War, and their own impracticability. These aspirations continue to be important to the terminology of United Nations operations. They encourage an emphasis on 'peace-making' or 'peace-keeping', not 'war'. This suggests an ability to control the commitment, and a limitation of effort that does not disrupt peace, or peacetime expectations of the relations between individuals and the state, but such terminology and assumptions could be misleading.

Nevertheless, changing assumptions are important. They indicate the de-legitimation not of war but of some forms of war. The notion that force should not be employed in order to alter frontiers was included in the United Nations Charter, and re-affirmed in a United Nations resolution of 1970. Aggressive war was also prohibited in the Charter. Combined with the idea of the sovereignty of the state, such notions have been important. They have not ended war or aggression, but they have changed their character. For example, seeking to overthrow a hostile government by supporting an insurrectionary movement is now far more effective than formally waging war. This is true even if there is a vast disproportion in the resources of the two states, such is the attitude towards aggressive warfare.

Such aggression was punished by international action when Iraq invaded Kuwait in 1990. The widespread nature of the coalition forces against Iraq was impressive, but so also was the overwhelming refusal of most of the world's states to recognize the Iraqi annexation. In part this was a consequence of America's leadership of the anti-Iraqi coalition; and it was no accident that the small number of states that recognized the annexation included such opponents of America as Cuba and Sudan. However, far more than this was involved. There was a widespread feeling that, in seeking to extinguish a state, Iraq had used violence in order to challenge the entire international system; that, in short, the pursuit of such politics by war was unacceptable. The American-led recourse was war, not blockade or any other expedient, but war under the mandate of the Security Council.

'Peace-making' or 'peace-keeping' would scarcely describe a clash between the USA and China, even if the cause of the conflict was an American response to Chinese military pressure on Taiwan; or indeed a Chinese response to American action to prevent an enhancement of the North Korean arsenal of advanced long-range weapons. Both are feasible, although in 2000 there were encouraging signs about a shift in North Korean policy. The Chinese showed with their intervention in Korea in 1950–53, their attack on India in 1962 and their invasion of Vietnam of 1979 that they were determined to assert their power when it seemed both necessary and possible. China's prosperity has helped make it more assertive, as has its sensitivity to criticism of its domestic situation, and the sense of the need to return to an intrinsic great power status that was compromised by the West in the nineteenth century.

More specifically, Russian weakness has both made China less vulnerable and has decreased its interest in good relations with the USA. This weakness has also been bad news for the Western alliance because it has encouraged neutralism in Europe. In particular, both French and German politicians continue to believe that it will be possible to manage Russia through some sort of partnership, and that this partnership reduces the need for co-operation with America. This is likely to be a major dividing point within both the European Union and NATO.

Russian weakness, and the absence of a universalist Russian ideology comparable to the liberal global interventionism of the USA, has made it most likely that China's opponent in any great power struggle will be the USA. This will also reflect America's specific interests in the West Pacific and, to a lesser extent, South-East Asia, and a more general concern to preserve the international order that it has created. In the case of China, there is also a tradition of American hostility, alongside that of a search for better relations. This tradition, and its location in terms of the political culture of the two states, provides both sides with a ready vocabulary for dispute. The 'comprehensive engagement' that America under President Clinton sought with China was designed to limit Chinese revisionism of the international order and included unsuccessful attempts to dissuade the Chinese from transferring advanced weaponry to hostile states.

Although China signed the Nuclear Non-Proliferation Treaty in 1992, it has only episodically observed its provisions. China provided parts used in uranium enrichment, M-11 missiles capable of carrying nuclear warheads, and information on how to build such warheads to Pakistan. China and the USA have clashed over these transfers and over American missile defence plans, and these arguments are likely to get worse. In 2000, the American government was warned that plans for a comprehensive missile defence system might lead the Chinese to increase dramatically their number of warheads, in order to be able to overcome whatever system the Americans could deploy. The entry of India and Pakistan into the ranks of the nuclear powers has made China's position look less secure and has increased the sensitivity of the issue of missile defence and deployment. Any increase in Chinese nuclear weaponry is likely to lead to a response by India and Pakistan.

China's long-term Versailles complex – the sense that it has been wronged by history – remains powerful. The return of Hong Kong and Macao removed prime irritants, but foreign concern about human rights within China, especially those of religious groups and Tibetans, is seen as unacceptable. Furthermore, the very fact of American power, let alone the ability of America to act to defend Taiwanese sovereignty, are not acceptable to Chinese policy-makers. This parallel with French attitudes after the Congress of Vienna in 1814–15 and German revisionism after the Peace of Versailles of 1919 serves as a powerful warning that the idea that the status quo should be the basis of future relations is inherently unacceptable to certain powers. It is perceived by them as both the cause and the symbol of international instability. Revisionist powers are generally seen as 'rogue' states when they seek to alter the situation by means outside those of peaceful negotiation, but, being realistic, such negotiation rarely serves the cause of revisionism, and to pretend otherwise would be complacent. As a consequence, revisionism is inherently a cause of instability, as is the response to it.

Aside from differences in South-East and East Asia, it is possible that China and the USA will clash in the future as a consequence of growing instability in the Pacific. Economic tensions in many of the island groups have exacerbated, and been accentuated by, ethnic tensions. In 2000 alone, this led to violent attempted coups in Fiji and the Solomon Islands. Since 1945, the Pacific has not been an international battlefield, as the defeat of Japan in World War II was followed by an American hegemony that was enhanced by the support of Australia and a re-armed Japan. It is possible, however, that as China becomes a stronger maritime state it will seek to challenge American interests. Whether successful or not, this will lead to a degree of instability in the Pacific and will further threaten relations between the two.

It is possible that Chinese membership, alongside Japan, South Korea and ASEAN, the Association of South-East Asian

Nations, in the ASEAN+3 network may temper China–USA tensions as many fellow-members have close ties with the West; but, in the long term, if global economic tensions become more serious, it may also provide China with a degree of regional support. Although capitalism (like democracy) has been seen as a force for peace, capitalist powers have fought each other, as in World War I, and, whatever their shared interests through trade, it is far from clear that a capitalist China will be a more welcome partner for a capitalist USA than Communist China was. Indeed, a capitalist China may find it easier to capitalize on East Asian disquiet with Western economic policies and financial hegemony, disquiet that grew after the 1997–98 financial crisis. The feeling that the West, through institutions such as the IMF, (rather than incompetent, if not corrupt, East Asian fiscal policies) was responsible for the crisis is deeply ingrained, and this has encouraged an East Asian search for economic autonomy. American and European protectionism will accentuate these tensions. The notion of a regional pact between China and Japan may appear incredible, but the European Union has brought France and Germany, and may bring Germany and Poland, together. However, China's ability to act as a regional leader will be undermined by continued suspicion of its intentions.

A conflict would test the military effectiveness not only of the USA and China, but also of their allies. It is far from clear that such a conflict would be settled by a technological lead, although it is also worth noting that, while such a remark would generally be seen as a warning against the inevitability of American victory, the Chinese themselves have made major advances in their military capability. In part, this has come from borrowing American capability, by trade, purchase and espionage. The relative ease of doing so, provided information can be obtained and the industrial infrastructure to permit production is present, serves as a reminder of the difficulty of maintaining a lead in technology. Indeed, the continued spread of advanced engineering and electronics will ensure that in the future the Western dominance of advanced weaponry and the relevant control systems will be increasingly challenged.

If advanced weaponry was used by America in an all-out conflict with China, it is not clear whether it could fulfil objectives or survive a rapid depletion rate. As in the Vietnam War, the timetable of conflict by the two sides might be very different, and such that the short-term high-intensity use of advanced technology by the Americans achieves devastating results, but without destroying the Chinese military system or the political determination to refuse American terms. In addition, the experience of recent conflicts, especially that with Serbia in 1999, suggests that 'just-in-time' procurement systems are inadequate. They provide neither sufficient weaponry nor the sense of confidence in reserves that is necessary for operational choice and for planning. This inadequacy is a product both of a financial stringency that mirrors constraints over manpower availability, and of the modernization of military technology which ensures high rates of obsolescence, and thus also discourages stockpiling.

A similar challenge will affect the USA in the event of any clash with a major Islamic power such as Iran, or Egypt were it to be taken over by fundamentalists. The Gulf War of 1990–91 is only a partial guide to the problems that might arise, because Iraq was isolated, the USA was aligned with Islamic states (Saudi Arabia and Syria), there was no attempt to overrun Iraq, and the situation elsewhere permitted a massive American commitment. More generally, the military challenge posed by Islamic assertiveness, whether fundamentalist or not, has been underrated because there is no single major Islamic state that enjoys power comparable to, say, India, let alone China or Russia. Furthermore, powerful rifts within Islam, not least between Shias and Sunnis, and between secularists and fundamentalists, are likely to continue, and may well become more savage.

Nevertheless, it is anticipated that by 2030 Muslims will

make up about 30 per cent of the world's population. Furthermore, as it has been claimed that religious and cultural clashes
and fault-lines are and will be the most probable cause of
conflict after the Cold War, so attention has focused on relations
between Islam and both Russia and Western powers. In
addition, Islam is also an issue in Central and South Asia,
sub-Saharan Africa, and the Balkans, an apparently bland
observation that is not intended to lessen its capacity for causing
conflict, or that of the response to Islamic assertiveness. Russian
concern to restore its influence within the states that were
formerly part of the Soviet Union will continue to lead to
conflict between Russian forces and Islamic fundamentalists, at
present in Tajikistan and Kirgizstan, and possibly in the future
in Uzbekistan.

Islam is not a united force, but there are common themes of
assertiveness. Much focuses on the rejection of the materialist
civilization and pluralist values associated with the West, as
well as rejection of its political and economic views, most particularly American support for Israel. Thus, in the event of
future conflict, there will be an ideological clash that will make
moderation in conflict and compromise in peace-making difficult. In South Asia, the nuclear armaments of Pakistan and India
are seen as Muslim bombs and Hindu bombs respectively. This
approach does not encourage disarmament.

The lesson of the Arab–Israeli conflict is very important here.
Although the Western-equipped and -organized Israeli military
was able to emerge victorious from individual wars, especially
the Six Days War of 1967, it found it difficult to triumph in the
conflict. This suggests a parallel in the event of any future
American–Islamic clash. Unlike Israel, however, the USA does
not have any contiguous boundaries with Islamic powers and
does not contain a substantial potentially hostile Islamic population (as Israel does within its pre-1967 boundaries, let alone
outside them). This may encourage a sense of controllability of
war on the part of American policy-makers: the 'we-can-fire-

cruise-missiles-and-switch-channels' syndrome. Howeve.
deeper and more sustained military engagement with Islam.
powers will face major challenges which will probably be
beyond American political capability. The American expeditionary force posture is not designed for occupation tasks and
commitments.

The contrast in time frames, and political cultures, between
the USA and non-Western powers, will not be the same in the
event of wars that do not directly involve Western powers, for
both military and political reasons. First, the tempo of military
activity will probably be lower and, thus, the rate of depletion of
military assets will be lower. Second, political expectations and
needs for a rapid result, while still pressing, will be less
powerful. In the next chapter, we will turn to how wars will be
fought. Suffice it to note here that the majority of international
wars in the future will probably continue not to involve the
leading military powers directly, although their weapons,
expertise and interests may all play a role, and are especially
likely to do so in Asia.

These wars are likely to be particularly common in sub-
Saharan Africa, a region where instabilities that, in part, arise
from the legacies of colonial rule, especially the mismatch of
political and ethnic boundaries, will continue to be exacerbated
by a resort to force that, in part, reflects the inability of states to
develop democratic mechanisms for the internal operation of
politics, and in part reflects the difficulty of moving past ethnic
constructions of politics. Post-colonial political structures and
practices have failed in their objectives of ensuring peace, prosperity and a government that is adequate or fair. Indeed, most
African states preside over public systems, whether of education or transport, health or finance, that are weak when they are
not in crisis. Their governments generally devote little attention
to these issues, and, instead, put a greater emphasis on the
politics of power, both domestic and international. Thus, in
2000 governments with acute internal problems, such as

Rwanda, Uganda and Zimbabwe, preferred to pursue foreign wars.

While such a preference is widespread, it is difficult to see the possibility of much long-term peace in sub-Saharan Africa. The colonial powers have gone, but, instead, countries are 'colonized' by regimes and their allies, for example the late President Mobutu in Zaire, or Robert Mugabe in Zimbabwe. Such regimes are frequently identified with tribal groups, although they tend to take their own, non-consultative definition of tribal interests.

States that comprise a number of often clashing ethnic groups, such as Angola, Congo, Kenya and Nigeria, will continue to be particularly unstable, and this will also affect their relations with each other. This instability may spread to South Africa, where tribal identity remains strong, and the role of the state as regulator and employer will encourage efforts to control its power. This will affect relations with neighbouring countries. In addition, attempts by states, such as Nigeria and South Africa, to act as regional hegemons will cause instability in Africa.

If, as already suggested, there will also be international instability leading to warfare in parts of Asia, the situation is less clear in Latin America. Here, American dominance may continue to restrict wars, and to restrain the activities of military governments. In 2000, American and Brazilian pressure on Paraguayan military leaders led them to thwart an attempted coup. The fact that, since the 1940s, wars have not been normative in Latin American politics may be very important for the future. Serious disputes, such as frontier disagreements between Argentina and Chile, have been settled without recourse to war, and there seems little reason to imagine that the situation will change.

However, alongside this optimistic vista, there is another that suggests that the pattern of intervention in the instabilities of neighbours seen in Central America in the 1980s may be repeated and may become more serious. The essential acceptance of state sovereignty that has characterized South American power politics might be eroded by a convergence of rising domestic pressures, not least drug-financed insurrection and terrorism, with opportunistic responses to the instability of neighbours. However, there are fewer contested frontiers in Latin America than in Africa. In addition, the Latin American militaries are more concerned with stability within their own countries than with war with their neighbours.

It is not clear that conflict in Latin America, whether international or domestic, would have a major impact on world politics. Such a statement begs the issue of how such a concept is to be defined and removed from subjective criteria. Nevertheless, in terms of geo-politics, the absence of close links between the Latin American states and rivalries between major global powers helps lessen the importance of conflict. There is nothing comparable to the Egypt or Syria–Soviet Union and Israel–USA relationships that helped to keep Middle Eastern conflicts at the forefront of attention during the Cold War, nor to American sponsorship of Pakistan and Soviet links with India in the same period. In South America, Communist attempts to build up powerful insurgency movements failed, American dominance remained powerful, whether the tide moved towards dictatorial or towards democratic regimes, and there was no key resource such as oil to provide occasion or funds for conflict, although, within states, drugs now provide that resource.

Looking ahead, it is difficult to anticipate any changes. Latin America may well be a vulnerable 'flank' for the USA, but the challenge may arise more from Latin America's relationship with sources of tension within the USA, such as economic competition, immigration and drug consumption, than from military or political factors. The fact that Cuba's strategic threat under Castro does not undermine American security at present suggests that it is inappropriate to envisage serious problems if, for example, Bolivia was ruled by an actively anti-American government.

Discussion of America, and proper acknowledgement of the role and importance of its military power and political leadership, should not lead to a neglect of the possible future importance in conflict and confrontation of both allies and of alliance structures. Here the Americans face a very uncertain future because the end of the Cold War, while leaving American hegemony even clearer, also weakened the cohesion of America's alliances, although this is not to suggest a lack of serious tensions in earlier periods. This is more true of Europe than East Asia, because fear of China and North Korea play, and will continue to play, a major role there, especially for Japan and Taiwan. In so far as Chinese–American tensions create a new bipolar geo-strategic confrontation, it will focus on East Asia.

In Europe, there is a continuing threat of instability in the Balkans and of confrontation with hostile powers in North Africa, but this will not cause a comparable maintenance of cohesion in relations with the USA. This is because the logic of NATO is challenged by the pretensions of the European superstate, and specifically because of a deep anti-Americanism in France, the state whose political conceptions will continue to be most influential in the European Union. France will be far more influential in the European Union than Britain, the major state that is happiest to adopt, and adapt to, American views. American hopes that closer British engagement with the European Union will lead to a European Union that is more responsive to the USA are naïve, although they largely account for American pressure for such engagement.

Furthermore, the expansion of NATO into eastern Europe threatens to weaken its cohesion, certainly in the event of any crisis involving commitments. For example, it is unclear whether guarantees to former Communist states would be supportable in the event of their being challenged by Russian-backed opposition movements that employed violence but were not supported by Russian troops. In the future, this may be a particular problem in the Baltic States, especially Latvia and, to a lesser extent, Estonia, as both have large Russian minorities. Similarly, NATO interest in the Caucasus may cause difficulties, with the views of Turkey, a NATO state and would-be European Union member, not being shared by other countries in either alliance.

The European Union itself showed in both the Gulf and Kosovo crises that it is unable to fulfil the expectations for political, let alone military, action that its proponents claim. This is likely to remain the case, and this weakness will probably affect the military situation in the eastern Mediterranean and more generally. The consequence will include strains in American multilateralism. The European Union's pretensions to independent policy-making will clash with the USA. So potentially will the enhanced capability that will flow from the projected 60,000-strong European Union deployment force, designed to be ready by 2003. Although this is intended in part to meet American demands that European powers take on a heavier defence burden, such a force is also intended to provide an out-of-NATO strike capacity that may lead to policy disagreements with the USA. The Americans want the European Union to be a reliable ally on American terms, in short complementary to the European arm of NATO. This, however, is wishful thinking.

It is possible to advance a more optimistic scenario, and to argue that arms controls and improved relations with Russia will lead to a more secure and stable Europe in which peacefulness will be the norm. Yet, such a scenario depends on overcoming traditional practices and concepts of state interest, and also on ensuring that when events help create crises, for example between Greece and Turkey, it is possible to maintain a systemic coherence, in short to prevent a breakdown of relations within Europe.

It is both more and less likely that this will be the case than was the situation a decade ago. Then, the collapse of the Soviet Union and its alliance system interacted with a Western globalism that seemed to leave scant role for traditional spheres of interest, and was thus a challenge to established notions of stability. However, the problems of such a policy have encouraged more caution of late, as shown in the acceptance in 2000 that Russia will maintain power by brutal means in the northern Caucasus. Furthermore, the very traditional assumption of geo-political and geo-economic blocs that the European Union represents will probably encourage a desire for stable neighbours and neighbouring blocs, although this policy has been less than successful in the Balkans.

Conversely, it is less likely than it was a decade ago that Russia will manage a successful transition to liberal capitalism and political pluralism. Instead, the strength of discontent within Russia may encourage a populist nationalism that threatens, intentionally or otherwise, to lead to conflict with neighbours. Furthermore, developments in what was Yugoslavia have underlined the risks both of conflict within European states and the involvement of other powers. Yugoslavia is not alone. The peaceful division of Czeckoslovakia into the Czech Republic and Slovakia removed one threat of civil unrest, but there remain powerful ethnic and regional tensions within Romania.

An understanding of the dangers of a weakening of NATO through the attempt to develop an independent European security identity serves as a reminder of the future role of contingencies. If the military history of, say, the 2020s is seen as likely to be different depending on whether NATO remains American-led and powerful, or not, with consequent influences on doctrine, strategy and force configuration, then the political contingencies that might determine this become far more important. They include political pressures within both the USA and Europe, as well as the impact of crises on relations between the two, for example conflict in the Balkans, the Middle East or the Far East. American nativism and European hostility to America might both be encouraged by xenophobic tendencies. Over the past century, wartime co-operation in the North Atlantic region was crucial both to the defeat of autocratic hegemonic tendencies in Europe and to the security of the USA. Such a scenario depends on continued effort and on circumstances, and is in no way inevitable.

Although it is unfashionable to say so, Western civilization was saved three times by the USA in the twentieth century, while one accepts of course that Germany in 1914 was not a threat comparable to the threats posed by Hitler and the Soviet Union, and that Britain played a far greater role than the USA in World War I. If a comparable challenge occurs, it should not be assumed that it will be possible to defeat it by the same means.

To refer to a comparable challenge may seem alarmist, but it is worth remembering that, hitherto, all post-war periods have been inter-war. Furthermore, hegemonic menace has a habit of responding to domestic strains and to international vacuums. If both are seen as inherent in political systems, then it becomes less easy to be confident about the future, unless the basis for a paradigm (fundamental) shift in the character of such systems can be deduced. That such a shift could be accomplished without major disruption, possibly including conflict, is unlikely. Certainly, the notion that future war will somehow be the fate of 'rogue' states and barbarous areas that cannot sustain statehood, while the West can choose isolation or 'peace-keeping', is overly complacent.

An understanding of the multiplicity of reasons for war breaking out is important, as is an understanding of the causes and, still more, the purposes of conflict to help to explain its conduct. It is to this that we now turn.

4 The Processes and Character of Future Conflict

> While the Gulf War was certainly a milestone in terms of international diplomatic and military co-operation, there are dangers in seeing it as a paradigm for all future military activity . . . Lower intensity peace support operations, for example, generate quite different challenges at all levels. The complexities of both high and low intensity operations can be made even more difficult when the forces involved are engaged in an asymmetric campaign.
>
> *British Maritime Doctrine* (2nd edition, 1999)

An understanding of the diversity of future wars helps to explain the range of future conflict. There will be no one type of war, and thus no one way of waging or winning war. Military goals will vary greatly, as will political contexts. The two are closely linked, although it is also important to note a degree of autonomy. While war may be the pursuit of politics, the institutions for, and demands of, conflict have exigencies of their own that do not readily respond to political requirements. We will begin by looking at 'high-tech' war, but then continue by stressing the need to consider other types of conflict.

Much of the assessment of future 'high-tech' war depends on two concepts: synergy (profitable combination) and information warfare. The former suggests that future success will hinge on the ability to achieve a successful synergy of land, air and sea forces. This requires the development of new organizational structures, as well as careful training of commanders and units, and appropriate systems of command, control, communication and information appraisal and analysis. These notions reflect not simply an awareness of the benefits for interdependency of ground, air and sea brought by technological developments, but also the experience of conflict from World War II on, especially the important examples of successful air–land, land–sea, air–sea and air–land–sea co-operation. It became clear, in particular, that air power was not an optional add-on but, instead, was important to operational success on land and sea.

Furthermore, the experience of land warfare has shown that technological advances worked best only if secured in a combined arms approach. Thus, in World War II, using tanks to try to revolutionize warfare was found to be of limited value in the face of 'counter-tank' practices, both the use of anti-tank weapons and the employment of tanks in mobile defence. The emphasis on the co-operation of armour with infantry and artillery that affects current thinking about future land conflict in large part stems from experience, and should be a warning against continued popular fascination with armour alone. To interject a personal note, an American tank colonel in conversation in 1997 responded to my query about the possibility of conflict over Taiwan by remarking that Taiwan was too small for his unit to operate in. The sense that the real world should conform to weaponry is flawed.

Doctrinal developments have also reflected particular conjunctions. The USA's promulgation of the concept of the Air Land Battle Doctrine in 1982 was designed to offset the particular problem of Soviet numerical superiority, but, looking ahead, it enshrined the notion that a successful combination of firepower and manoeuvre would be a vital addition to positional defence, and that this would require an effective synergy of land and air. In addition, Air Land looked ahead in its emphasis on a level of conflict, and thus planning, in war between tactics and strategy. This operational level has already played a major role in Soviet planning and is likely to play a more important role in future military doctrine and planning. It reflects the transformation of strategy.

Advanced technology, and a sense that technology will continue to advance, and that this has to be planned for, greatly contributes to ideas of synergetical warfare. They reflect an awareness of the need for a more sophisticated command and planning environment, and also a need to do more than simply respond to the possibilities created by new weapons. Instead of treating these in isolation, their impact is to be multiplied by careful co-operation.

There is no shortage of plans for new weapons. The Americans plan to employ stealthy attack aircraft and 'smart' guided weapons fired from stand-off platforms. Laser-guided projectiles and programmed cruise missiles are intended to attack ground targets, while advanced aircraft will win air superiority. Stealth technology will permit the penetration of opposing air defences, obliging enemies to retain more aircraft at home. Looking further ahead, there has been discussion of the use of high-speed aircraft capable of 'skipping' on the upper atmosphere and of transporting troops anywhere in the world within two hours.

Such technology has to be impacted within new processes to ensure effectiveness, not least at the expense of the use of similar weaponry by opponents. Co-ordination will be made possible by computer networking, information assessment through spy satellites and other important sensors, such as AWACS aircraft, and the use of Global Positioning Systems. The compartmentalization and secrecy of intelligence gathering and dissemination processes and agencies will need to be broken down, a task requiring a powerful shift in agency cultures. At the same time, the importance of these information supplies will ensure that much effort has to be put into making them secure from both interception and disruption. The risk of the latter will increase as real-time information is integrated into decision-making at lower unit levels, for example targeting by individual tanks, guns and soldiers.

This serves as a reminder of the potential vulnerability that will come from improved systems, and this vulnerability will need to be built in to any assessment of capability. However advanced, modern communication systems are vulnerable to a number of disruption mechanisms as well as to surveillance. This is especially true in the confusion of combat.

Information co-ordination, furthermore, is more difficult in practice than in theory, especially in high-tempo situations. This affects not only the movement of information to individual units, and its analysis with reference to their needs, but also the relationship between planning and operations. As it is the case that the speed of communications will increase, and this will also be true of opposing forces, so the pressures of simultaneity will be exacerbated. It is by no means clear how far command and control, which ultimately depends on human decision-making, will be enhanced or compromised by the massive and rapid flow of information. The visual understanding of quantities of information, much of it in three dimensions, will also pose problems. Furthermore, it is unclear whether the resulting control will focus on commanders able to direct the moves and fire of distant vehicles, platforms and soldiers, or on the latter – able to have continuous and instantaneous access to all relevant combat zone information.

In Western planning, there will also be an emphasis on the sea as a sphere for manoeuvre and as a base area. This will reflect the problems that civilian opposition and insurrectionary movements pose for the use of land as a military base, and the geo-political shifts produced by the end of colonial bases, and by political sensitivities over the deployment of troops in the territory of allies. This will continue to affect the Western forces. For example, pro-Western Arab states are sensitive about the deployment of American troops, and in the Kosovo crisis of 1999 there was considerable hostility in Greece, a NATO power, to the use of the country for transshipment. In Asia, the Americans face similar problems, in both Japan and the Philippines, as they have also done in Pakistan and New Zealand.

As a consequence, the geo-politics of alliances has changed fundamentally, a shift that can be seen as a counterpart to the Revolution in Attitudes to the Military (RAM) already discussed. There is no reason to believe that this process will be reversed, but, instead, every reason to anticipate that it will be accentuated. It may, in time, affect the use of European and Australian facilities by the USA.

Indeed, the expansion of the European Union to include states with neutralist traditions, such as Austria, Finland and Sweden, may be followed by further expansion to include more, for example Malta or (Greek) Cyprus. This may encourage a hostility to the use of the European Union as a base area for American forces or operations.

The possibilities of sea-based forces have been enhanced by new technology. Basing aircraft on ships and, later, ballistic missiles on submarines was followed by the development in sea-based guided tactical missiles. Active naval construction programmes continue. They are designed to enhance the capability of individual units. Launched in 1998, France's 40,000-ton nuclear-powered aircraft carrier, *Charles de Gaulle*, is the largest European warship in decades. In 1998, Britain announced plans to build two carriers of a similar size, each costing £1 billion, and Italy approved a small carrier with amphibious assault capabilities.

Aside from the sea as a platform for mounting bomb and missile attacks, there will continue to be an emphasis on the potential for amphibious operations, whether in attack, in reinforcement, or for the defence or withdrawal of interests and people. Amphibious operations offer the seizure of the initiative, manoeuvrability, and combination of different arms sought by modern strategists. Their value will remain high because so much of the world's population and economic power is located on or close to littorals (coastal areas), and because so many states have coastlines and are therefore vulnerable. Thus the sea was used as the initial approach route for the British intervention in

Sierra Leone in 2000. At the present moment, there is much work on the development of medium-sized amphibious vessels.

A stress on amphibious capability will also be important because only a small number of states possess, and will possess, it. Indeed, a sea-based strategy will be of use to naval powers not only because they will have the capability, but also because it will enable them to emphasize their distinctiveness, and thus to gain an important psychological advantage.

The relative safety of the sea will maintain the contrast between military capability on land and at sea that will be so important in future military capability and conflict. Irregular forces operate far less at sea, and this will continue to be the case. There will continue to be high levels of piracy off parts of South-East Asia and, to a lesser extent, in the Caribbean, and these may spread, for example in African coastal waters, but such vessels will not be able to threaten the warships of major powers, and nor indeed will they seek to do so, because the economic rationale of piracy will depend on avoiding such confrontation.

Furthermore, although modern warships and those on the drawing board are soft-skinned compared to their predecessors, and certainly not armoured behemoths, their protection will be enhanced by sophisticated surveillance systems linked, in particular, to anti-aircraft and anti-missile weaponry, and their range will be extended by aircraft, helicopters and missiles. At sea, it is, and will continue to be, easier to distinguish and assess other units than on land. As a consequence, it will be possible to avoid the situation on land in which guerrillas will be indistinguishable from the civilian population.

The sea, in short, will be known, although the application of stealth technology to warships will pose a problem. As a consequence of the range provided by aircraft, helicopters and missiles, ships will be far better able to mount attacks on hostile powers than their predecessors. In addition, the 'transition costs' of amphibious operations will be greatly lessened as the point of contact (and emphasis) of sea-based attacks will cease to be simply the coastal landing zone: the littoral will replace the coastline. Naval power will offer reach, mobility and logistical independence. It will provide a dynamic quality that will be lacking from fixed overseas garrisons.

Naval capability will thus offer a military substitute for colonial possessions. This will be particularly appropriate for the world's leading naval power, the USA, because its political culture does not make colonial rule acceptable. This is also true of the other major naval powers, with the exception of China. The use of naval power in support of a seizure of Taiwan would be presented by the Chinese as a reunion, but it would also have, at least in part, an imperialist character. Elsewhere, however, it is on land that China pursues colonialism – in Tibet and Xianjiang – not at sea.

The cost of major vessels and of naval infrastructure is such that naval power will become even more of a high-cost exercise. In part, this reflects the needs for very advanced electronics. These are largely a response to the extent to which surface vessels became more vulnerable last century as a consequence of the development of submarines and of air power. It has become necessary to devise counter-measures and also to ensure that the various forces that can operate on, over and under the sea combine effectively. This will become even more the case if the hopes of protagonists of sea-to-land capability are to be realized.

The limited number of states with any major naval effectiveness suggests that the sea will essentially be used for sea-to-land operations rather than contested between marine powers. Nevertheless, the possibilities of naval conflict have been enhanced by the increase in the number of naval powers, as well as the naval plans of a number of states. Naval shipbuilding has developed in newly industrialized countries, especially Argentina, Brazil and India, there has been an arms race in East and South-East Asia, and wealthy states that lack large navies have proved willing to buy advanced naval vessels. Thus, for example, Iran has acquired sophisticated Russian submarines.

It is possible to point to particular issues that may lead to the use of such vessels. For example, disputes over islands and territorial waters in the South China Sea involve the states that border the sea, especially the struggle over the Spratlys. Episodic fighting in the sea since 1974 involving China and Vietnam, and confrontations involving, in addition, Malaysia, the Philippines and Taiwan, have fuelled naval build-ups in the region, although hitherto they have not led to war.

It is unclear how far this is likely to remain the case. The Western Pacific/East Asian littoral zone is one of the most volatile regions in world power politics. In geo-political terms it is a fault-line, akin to that between two tectonic plates, in this case the Pacific, which is currently under American control, and the East Asian littoral, where American interests are challenged.

Such an instability can be seen as likely to restrain war. The close proximity of heavily armed forces might lead to a caution bred of fear about likely escalation, but it could also lead to war by accident, or encourage the search for apparently 'safer' topics for conflict. Naval clashes in the South China Sea might well serve as a prime example of these, enabling China to win a contained conflict with a state far less powerful than the USA. There are also in this area the resource concerns mentioned in the previous chapter, in particular oil.

It is possible that the increase in the number of states with submarines will ensure that submarine warfare and anti-submarine capability will play a greater role in future confrontations than in the conflicts of the 1990s. The security of deployment enjoyed by Western forces in the Gulf and Kosovo Wars (as earlier in the Korean and Vietnam Wars) may not be readily replicated. Indeed, a modest outlay in submarines by hostile powers may oblige Western forces to regard their deployment routes as an active combat zone. This would have an important impact on naval resources, which have been stretched thin by the rundown in the number of units. It is worth thinking back to the Falkland War of 1982 and considering how many warships the British would have had available for operations round the Falkland Islands had they also had to protect routes right the way back to the British Isles from the threat of Argentinian submarine attack.

Such a threat may well serve further to encourage long-distance deployment by air, but this requires safe landing zones; on the ground, aircraft are very vulnerable to attack. In addition, the use of aircraft is restricted by the weather. Reliance on air also makes it even more likely that future distant deployments will not include sizeable armoured forces. Tanks require much space and a formidable support and supply system. Tanks can be moved in aircraft, but it is likely that an enhanced reliance on long-distance deployment and re-supply by air will contribute to the growing marginality of armour. This will be a marked contrast with the situation during the Cold War. The contrast will also mark a major shift in popular assumptions about the character and weaponry of land conflict.

If the sea is likely to be primarily important in terms of a base for force projection onto land and for logistical and transport capability, then it is still necessary to consider how far future land conflict will reflect present patterns. Much of the problem arises from different judgements of the latter. As planning and training for future wars in large part reflects the 'lessons' of the past, then the controverted nature of the latter is particularly important. This was especially true of the Gulf War of 1990–91, because it witnessed conflict on land and in the air; but was also true of the Kosovo War of 1999.

Learning from past performance is important as it offers an assessment of current capability. In the absence of evidence of such performance, it is difficult to judge capability. For this reason, the continuing ability of states to understand their relative position may depend on the frequency of conflict in the future. This will cause a significant problem because large-scale conflict is (it is hoped) likely to be infrequent, and thus it will be very difficult for militaries to realize deficiencies in time to do anything about them: major war may well be an event, rather than, as in 1689–1713, 1739–63, 1792–1815 and 1914–45, a sequence.

The Gulf War has played a particularly important role in current discussion because it led to what could be presented as a clear-cut victory, because it was played out in the full blaze of publicity, and because offensive campaigns have always attracted more analysis than their defensive counterparts. Furthermore, the Gulf War appears to be a model of an important type of future conflict because it opposed an American-led coalition to a 'rogue' state.

The Gulf War was widely presented as a triumph for technology and for doctrines based on advanced weaponry. As pictures of precision bombs and missiles destroying their targets were endlessly repeated on television, the war helped to resurrect popular and air force confidence in the capability and impact of air power following its apparent failure in the Vietnam War. The Gulf War tested the doctrine and practice of the Air Land Battle, and did so at the moment when American analysis and preparation for what was termed the Revolution in Military Affairs (RMA) were coming together.

In the Gulf War, the Americans employed high technology in reconnaissance, offence, defence and communications, and all were hailed as anticipations of the future nature of conflict, not least as advertisements for particular weapons systems that would be employed to fight future wars. Reconnaissance was not separate from offence or defence, but was closely linked to the weapons available for both. Satellite surveillance was employed to track Iraqi missile launches, as well as to guide individual Allied units. Near-real-time information and communication provided many more opportunities for individual units on the ground to take decisions, and led to pressure for real-time information. Allied tanks successfully employed precise positioning devices interacting with American satellites in a Global Positioning System. Satellite imagery was responsible for the rapid production of photo-maps.

Information was also important to the missile assaults by Tomahawk cruise missiles. These made use of the precise prior mapping of target and traverse in order to follow predetermined courses to targets that were actualized for the weapon as grid references. Thus digital terrain models of the intended flight path provided precise long-distance firepower.

Firepower was also enhanced by other methods. Thermal-imaging laser-designation systems were employed to guide bombs to their targets, and tanks also made effective use of thermal-imaging sights. Other high-tech weaponry included B-2 Stealth bombers, which were able to bomb Baghdad, one of the most heavily defended cities in the world, with total impunity and considerable precision. Stealth technology did indeed minimize radar detection. Patriot anti-missile missiles were used to protect bases in Saudi Arabia from Iraqi attack. Unmanned air vehicles, electronic countermeasures and fuel-air explosions were employed.

The attack weaponry was supported by sophisticated and complex control systems designed to help maintain the pace of the attack. Compared to earlier conflicts, target acquisition and accuracy were effective, although the defensive character of the target and the desert nature of the terrain was a great help. The Iraqis were defeated with heavy casualties and, proportionally, even greater losses of equipment, while their opponents lost very few men or equipment.

Thus the Gulf War appeared to show the way ahead. 'Rogue states', however well armed, would be defeated by well-trained American-led forces capable of using advanced weaponry in an effective fashion and to a timetable. Yet, the war was capable of a very different analysis, which also looked ahead to suggest that the nature of future warfare would be less comforting for protagonists of the RMA and for those who suggested that American hegemony would be relatively unproblematic. First and foremost, there were doubts about the effectiveness of high-tech weaponry, and thus about the impact of a future capability advantage based on technological strength and operating through such weaponry. For example, subsequent analysis indicated that the Stealth planes, Tomahawk and Patriot missiles, and laser-guided bombs did less well than was claimed at the time. In particular, their much-lauded accuracy was less manifest in combat conditions than had been anticipated, especially that of the Patriots, as also of the Soviet-supplied Iraqi Scud missiles.

Furthermore, command and control proved unequal to the fast tempo of the conflict, unsurprisingly so. Indeed, the system buckled under the combined strain of its very complexity and of this tempo. Air Land battle proved more difficult in practice than in theory, not least due to the problems of synchronizing air and land forces under fast-moving combat conditions. The deficiencies of air and missile attack attracted most attention, but other limitations were also revealed. For example, on the ground, supporting artillery fire suffered from deficiencies, including a lack of adequate ammunition, and poor integration at unit level.

In addition, analysis of the war suggested that factors other than weapons and their use were crucial. Much of the success of the Allied coalition was arguably due not to respective weaponry, but to Allied, principally American, fighting quality, unit cohesion, leadership and planning, and to Iraqi limitations in all four and in other respects. In addition, the Iraqis surrendered mobility and the initiative by entrenching themselves to protect their conquest of Kuwait. The Allied task and the Iraqi response were suited to what has been seen as the American systematic, production-line approach to warfare, and failed to encourage attention to the limitations of the latter.

In the Gulf War, there were claims of a Western failure of nerve that allowed President Saddam Hussein of Iraq to survive the crisis; in short an echo of the argument that domestic, political and media pressures subvert the Western military, an argument much voiced in analysis of the Vietnam War.

However, no comparable lack of resolve was shown by the Israelis in their operations in Lebanon over the last quarter-century. Major operations in 1978, 1982, 1994 and 1996 were thwarted not by Israeli politics, but by the intractable nature of the opposition. At one level, a high-tech 'solution' was possible – Lebanon could have been turned into a nuclear wasteland – but such a war-brought holocaust was not an option, and, instead, the Israelis learned the deficiencies of waging war using advanced conventional weaponry.

Problems with advanced weaponry were again extensively discussed during, and after, the Kosovo War of 1999, a conflict that was fought out in the full glare of attention, and amidst considerable controversy about the effectiveness and potential of particular weapon systems. Reiterated NATO claims about the destructiveness of air power proved greatly misleading. Far more Serb tanks survived than had been anticipated, and this suggested that the use of air power against less prominent units, for example mortars, machine guns or individual soldiers, would have been even less successful. The Serbs, employing simple and inexpensive camouflage techniques, succeeded in preserving most of their equipment. Their eventual retreat seems to have been due to Russian pressure, to the maintenance of NATO cohesion, and to the threat of a NATO land attack, rather than to the lengthy air offensive which involved 10,000 strike sorties.

The report produced by the British National Audit Office in 2000 on British operations the previous year depicted a series of serious limitations. These included serious shortages of specialists for the Royal Air Force and major operational problems. On cloudy days, the planes were unable to identify targets and were grounded. Ironically, this prevented an excessive depletion of guided bombs. In addition, many bombs mounted on aircraft were unable to survive the shocks of take-offs. Furthermore, many missiles carried by Royal Navy Harrier jump jets became useless after a few sorties due to heat and vibration damage. Furthermore, Tornado GR4 jets were reportedly unable to drop precision-guided bombs effectively. These jets also proved deficient in operations over Iraq due to the consequences of heat. This offered an ironic warning about the deficiencies of globalism, for state-of-the-art weaponry was assumed to be effective all over the world. There were also serious problems with British communications. Enemy forces were readily able to monitor British radio communications, and the army also lacked secure voice and data communication links to the UK. A lack of lift capacity led to a reliance on Russian-built Antonovs hired from private contractors but whose use was dependent on Russian certification. The SA80 rifle, the main infantry weapon, was found to be faulty. In addition, there was a shortage of medical supplies, and of accommodation.

It is, of course, possible to speculate as to the likely effectiveness of an Allied land attack on the Serbs in Kosovo in 1999, had one been mounted. It would certainly have posed a questionmark against the tactical effectiveness of Western forces. For example, close air support would have been difficult in cloudy weather, and much of the terrain and ground cover were not suitable for Allied attack, and, instead, would have favoured the defence. In practice, there would probably have been more close-quarter fighting than in the Gulf War, a greater reliance on infantry, and, probably, a greater use of artillery, rather than tanks or air power, in order to weaken hostile positions. The result, a close interaction of infantry and artillery, would not have been anachronistic, but would have been a reminder of the need to be cautious before assuming that any future operations by leading military states would necessarily focus on air power and, if on the ground, armour or even heavily mechanized combat units.

In many respects, the infantry–artillery combination will probably remain the crucial military option in land operations. This point needs underlining as it is so much at variance with the bulk of modern assumptions. It is necessary anyway to stress the atypicality of the Gulf and Kosovo Wars, while bearing in mind that no war is typical. In Kosovo, there was no ground fighting between Western and Serb forces, although there was much fighting between the Kosovo Liberation Army and the Serbs. In the latter, the classic factors of territorial control and denial were contested on land, and the conflict did not measure up to the paradigms of information warfare. Instead, it was closer to the notions of future warfare as a savage dialectic of guerrilla operations and brutal counterinsurgency. Prior to the Western air assault, the tasking that faced the Serb military and paramilitary forces was defined in these terms, and these have to be used in assessing their capability.

An interesting parallel was provided the following year when Ethiopia invaded Eritrea. As with many 'Third World' conflicts, it is difficult to be precise about events, but the Ethiopians benefited from superior air power, better armour (Russian T-72 tanks), and greater numbers, but found the Eritreans fought well, taking advantage of the terrain.

To return to the importance of infantry, in the Gulf War, where attacking infantry played only a limited role, the Allies' armour was able to exploit the static nature of their opponent and their exposed flank, and also to use air power, and did both effectively. There was relatively little role for the Allied infantry, but there would have been far more had it not been possible to outflank the Iraqis.

The air assault in the Kosovo conflict offered scant guidance to the likely nature of fighting on the ground had the Western forces attacked and should not be used to proclaim the obsolescence of ground forces concerned with territorial control. In addition, had there been a ground attack, supply routes would have been crucial to any Western advance, and they would have had to have been protected. Deep-space attacking operations could not have done that, and it is important not to exaggerate the consequences of disorientating opponents by such moves.

Yet, as already argued, this approach hardly suits with much contemporary discussion. Why? My analysis focuses, in part, on treating the belief in the RMA as symptomatic of a set of cultural and political assumptions that tell us more about modern Western society than they do about any objective assessment of military options. This is not surprising. We should not assume an objectivity in military discussion and analysis somehow removed from the rest of society.

Instead, the RMA acts as a nexus for a range of developments and beliefs, including an unwillingness to accept conscription, a very low threshold for casualties, an assertion of Western superiority, and the ideology of machinism. The last is crucial. In a machine age, worth is defined in terms of machines. They, rather than ideas or beliefs, are used to assert superiority over other humans, as well as over the environment. Furthermore, change is the characteristic of machinism. Machines are designed to serve a purpose and can be improved. They have a limited life, life understood as being at the cutting edge of applicability, and are intended for replacement. A stress on machines leads to an underrating of infantry. Furthermore, the stress is on moving machines. This leads to an underrating of the role of artillery.

Such a process is not new. It can be seen also in the remembrance of military success. A prominent instance occurs with World War I. It is frequently claimed that tanks broke the impasse on the Western Front in 1918. In fact, their role has been exaggerated. Effective infantry–artillery co-ordination was far more important to the Allied success. This, however, lacked, and lacks, the glamour of the concept of the tank advance, and also does not appear as the turning point beloved of military commentators. Looking to the past for examples, in this fashion, is valuable, as modern analysts about contemporary and future conflict often show the same characteristics as their predecessors.

Translated into warfare, machinism assumes that capability will vary greatly between powers, producing a ready hierarchy, that capability will change, and that this change will be easily assessed. This approach readily lends itself to the notion of perfectability, and to the concept of paradigm leaps forward.

Thus the RMA is an expression of the modern secular technological belief-system that is prevalent in the West. This easily meshes with theories of modernization that rest on the adoption of technological systems, and serves powerful psychological needs: it is particularly crucial to Americans that this is an American military revolution, not least because it permits a ranking in which America is foremost, and all other powers – opponents, neutrals and even allies – are weak and deficient. The RMA meets the American need to believe in the possibility of High Intensity Conflict and of total victory, and appears to counter the threats posed by the spread of earlier technologies, such as long-range missiles and atomic warheads, of new ones, such as bacteriological warfare, and of whatever may follow. It keeps the Americans ahead. Furthermore, the RMA can serve to support a range of Western political strategies, more particularly the doctrine, politics and military strategy, both of isolationists and of believers in collective security.

However, it is also necessary to be cautious in suggesting too much coherence and consistency in the idea of an RMA. A less harsh view than that just outlined can be advanced if the RMA is presented as a doctrine designed to meet political goals, and thus to shape or encourage technological developments and tactical suppositions accordingly, rather than to allow technological constraints to shape doctrine, and thus risk the danger of inhibiting policy.

Allowing for this, much modern discussion does seem to suggest a technology-driven warfare. Advocates of the RMA have progressed to talking about 'space control' and the 'empty battlefield' of the future, where wars will be waged for 'information dominance' – in other words, control of satellites, telecommunications and computer networks. The American military refers to information grids and networks that must be safeguarded in wartime, and hostile ones that must be destroyed. Integrated communications technologies are designed to enhance offensive and defensive information warfare capability. Better communications enable both more integrated fire support and the use of surveillance to permit more accurate targeting.

Western economic growth gives substance to such ideas, because it makes it easier to afford investment in new military systems, or, at least, the development of earlier ones. Furthermore, in planning for future weaponry and warfare, there has been an understandable tendency to develop the ideas and weapons of the 1990s. The emphasis has been on precision, mobility and an avoidance of risk. For example, signature reduction is designed to reduce vulnerability to targeting.

Many of these notions are similar to those that earlier influenced planning for nuclear attack. Given the widespread devastation that the latter would have caused, such a remark might appear surprising, but the pinpointing of nuclear missile silos in order to provide accurate targeting for precise attacks was very important in nuclear strategy.

Today, planning for future weaponry reveals a stress on cheaper, unmanned platforms to replace reconnaissance and attack aircraft. Whether termed UAVs (unmanned aerial vehicles) or RPVs (remotely piloted vehicles), these platforms are designed to take the advantage of missiles further by providing mobile platforms from which they can be fired or bombs dropped. Platforms do not require on-site crew and thus can be used without risk to the life or liberty of personnel. As a consequence, they can be low flying, as the risk of losses of pilots to anti-aircraft fire has been removed. In addition, at least in theory, the logistical burden of air power is reduced. So also is the cost, as unmanned platforms are less expensive than manned counterparts, and there are big savings in pilot training. Unmanned platforms should also be more compact and 'stealthy', i.e. less easy to detect. The acceleration and manoeuvrability of such platforms would be no longer limited by G-forces that would render a pilot unconscious. Over Kosovo in 1999, unarmed drones were used extensively for surveillance in order to send information on bomb damage and refugee columns.

In 2000, the American Air Force announced experiments with dropping bombs from unmanned aircraft. The 26-foot Predator, used over Kosovo in 1999, will be adapted to carry two satellite-guided 'smart' bombs, as a prelude to future tests with larger bombs or missiles. The planes will have an operating radius of 500 miles, a flight duration of up to 40 hours, a cruising speed of 80 mph, and a normal operating altitude of 15,000 feet. Designed to destroy air-defence batteries and command centres, these planes could be used in areas contaminated from chemical or germ warfare. The software is planned to be able to tell if the intended target has moved close to civilians and to suggest, accordingly, a change of plan.

The replacement of Tomahawks by 'jumbo cruise missiles' is similarly designed to enhance versatility without any surrender to vulnerability. Tanks are increasingly seen as obsolescent, in that their range is limited, their durability is affected by terrain, and their expense is high, both in terms of purchase and of maintenance. As a consequence, there has been talk of cruise missiles replacing tanks. At sea, aircraft carriers are seen as becoming less necessary, as missiles replace aircraft. As a consequence, there has been talk of their replacement by 'arsenal ships'. The capability of such weapons is to be enhanced by designing them to work within systems or networks that bring together dispersed units and different types of weapons, for example from different environments.

America is at the forefront of such technology, although it is not alone in its development goals, and, in order to recoup some of the cost, is likely to try to sell advanced weapons to allies. It is difficult to control this process. For example, in 2000, the Americans threatened action if Israel sold to China an American-supplied airborne radar system that could be used against Taiwan.

It may be asked how far it is possible to reconcile such weaponry with some of the geo-strategic speculation about future conflict. In particular, the stress on a likely American search for Russian co-operation against China presupposes, at least in part, a more traditional emphasis on land frontiers and propinquity. Such a basis for operations would still benefit from manoeuvrable and deep-penetration forces, but there would be no need, on the part of the Russians, for sea-based platforms with their logistical and space constraints and their degree of vulnerability. Given that most discussion of future war between major powers focuses on American, or at least Western forces, weaponry and doctrine, it is worth noting that it could also be between China and Russia. Whereas, in the 1960s, this would have found the Chinese stronger on numbers than weapons, the situation is different now.

Furthermore, in contrast to the emphasis in modern discussion of a lack of Western interest in territorial expansion, it is possible to see a very different situation in this case. There is a border that the Chinese have reason to want reversed. Russia gained the Amur region in 1858 and the Ussuri region in 1860. The Treaty of Beijing of 1860 delimited the new frontier , but was wrung from the Chinese in a year of defeat and humiliation: Beijing was occupied by Anglo-French forces in 1860. While not as humiliating and deeply ingrained in Chinese consciousness as the loss of Hong Kong to the British, this is unfinished business. In addition, regaining these territories would undermine the Russian position in Siberia, providing opportunities for enhanced Chinese influence and resource acquisition, whether in co-operation with, or in opposition to, the Russians.

Were it to occur, such a conflict is likely to be waged without the concern to minimize civilian and military losses that characterizes Western operations. There is likely to be a similar emphasis on mobility, but also a greater reliance on the attritional characteristics of firepower, and a greater willingness to engage in frontal attacks (provided that there is a firepower advantage), rather than searching for a vulnerable flank. The vulnerability of the Russian Far East to Chinese attack from Manchuria makes the situation very different from operating into Siberia. For the Chinese, an advance overland to the Sea of Okhotsk in order to cut off the region, followed by the capture of Vladivostok, might appear a tempting 'small war', especially if the Russians were already engaged in Central Asia and the Caucasus.

Mobility indeed is the goal of the militaries of the future. It is seen as the best way to fight if conflict breaks out in established zones of tension, and the best way to respond to other challenges. Thus, the Weizsäcker commission on the future of the German military that reported in 2000 recommended that the size of the German rapid deployment forces rise from 60,000 to 140,000 men. This trend towards mobility has been led by the USA, followed by Britain. In Western Europe, France and, to a lesser extent, Spain and Italy are following, and elsewhere in the world those states that seek a distant projection of their power are also seeking to do so.

The weaponry being developed by the USA and other states as the tools of future war is designed to ensure what are termed dominant manoeuvre, precision engagements, full dimensional protection, focused logistics and information warfare. All of these are seen as the goals and methods of future military structures, and particular organizational forms and weapons are presented as intended to serve these ends, rather than simply moulding the structures or methods for a world of joint operations.

Planners increasingly think in terms of the redundancy of traditional service distinctions. There has been a proliferation of 'joint' organizations. In America, these include the creation in 1992 of an Expeditionary Warfare Division in the office of the Chief of Naval Operations and, more generally, the Goldwater-Nichols Department of Defense Reorganization Act of 1986. This strengthened the position of the Chairman of the Joint

Chiefs of Staff and established a joint acquisition system. In Britain, the plethora of joints include the Joint Rapid Deployment Force, the permanent Joint Headquarters, and the Joint Services Command and Staff College. Joint institutions provide powerful advocates for new doctrine and plans, such as the American *Joint Vision 2010* plan.

Joint institutions and planning has many uses. Given that particular weapons systems and strategies are advocated and discussed in terms of doctrines that reflect the composition and culture of particular military institutions, there is much to be said for pressing the case for unity and giving it institutional form and focus. Furthermore, traditional distinctions between the services have generally been more fluid and affected by circumstances than they may appear or as they have often been presented, and there is no reason why there should not be even more fluidity in the future. That is not the same, however, as unitary tasking. While the abolition of the notion of separate services may have some value for conflict between conventional forces, there is a world of difference between the task of counter-insurgency operations on urban streets and that of mounting, or responding to, long-range missile attacks on hostile states.

The latter point serves as a reminder of another drawback of the RMA analysis. It purports to offer a means to total victory, providing the opportunity for a universal war-fighting doctrine that, however, offers very little for the Low Intensity Conflict that was the combat norm during the Cold War, has become even more so subsequently, and is likely to continue to be the case. The Americans have been able to take advantage of developments in military doctrine and weaponry in order to retain their military lead, but one needs to remember that aggregate capability is not the same as capability or success in particular scenarios.

In particular, there is a danger that the conviction of the value of high technology that lies at the centre of the RMA will serve as an apparent substitute for a political willingness to commit troops.

Furthermore, it also threatens to serve as a cover for a failure to develop effective territorial control and counterinsurgency doctrines and practices, to conceive of a strategy for successful long-term expeditionary operations, and to work within the difficult context of alliance policy-making and strategic control.

Before turning to this type of warfare, it is, however, important to note that there are scenarios between that of territorial control/counterinsurgency warfare and that of conflict between two high-tech forces. In particular, the acquisition of advanced weaponry by so-called 'rogue' states creates the prospect of confrontation, even conflict, in which there is no equality of armament, but both sides rely on technology or the threat of its use. Concern about developing Chinese, North Korean, Iranian, Iraqi, Libyan, Syrian and other long-range missile capability, including the growth of Chinese and Iranian submarine forces, and the surprise test-firing by North Korea in August 1998 of a three-stage Taepodong I rocket over Japan into the Pacific, and the spread of weapons of mass destruction has altered the balance of concern. There has been a marked and public renewal in American interest in a comprehensive missile defence system and a national missile defence scheme (NMD).

This has also led to discussion in Europe, Japan, Taiwan and other countries about the need for a similar system, or about how best to respond to American policies and their likely consequences for alliances with America and for relations with Russia and China. Thus, new missile-defence schemes may produce a new geo-politics. In Europe there has been concern about a 'decoupling' by the USA, as only it, not Europe, would be protected, in so far as protection is possible. It would require a more ambitious NMD to protect Europe and it would also be much harder to persuade Russia to accept so extensive a revision of the Anti-Ballistic Missile Treaty of 1972 (SALT 1). A similar threat to NATO has been seen in Canada, although it is likely that proximity will ensure that American defences cover most of the highly populated areas.

The possession of advanced weaponry by 'rogue' states enables them to offset the strength of the West's non-nuclear military capability. It provides both a valuable tool with which to intimidate local rivals and an important means for counter-deterrence. The latter involves removing the overhang of Western nuclear and non-nuclear power. This very much challenges American interests, and exacerbates American concern that the failings of international bodies to maintain an orderly world will be mirrored by deficiencies in the American force profile. Thus the ability of America to protect its interests and allies seems limited unless America's defensive system is enhanced, as well as re-directed from a focus on the Soviet Union to include the threat from other states.

Concern about the range of the missiles deployed in hostile states will exacerbate the sense of vulnerability. This has a major impact on the politics of military preparedness. In essence, politicians and the public have a low tolerance of vulnerability and fear. This leads to demands for a secure and comprehensive defence system, but, in practice, no system is likely to be both. Although satellite surveillance and real-time communications have improved, and will continue to do so, the speed of a missile attack, and its likely combination with decoys and with satellite and communication disruption, pose many problems. Decoys are a particular problem as, outside the atmosphere, there is no air resistance, and objects of different weights and shapes therefore behave in the same way, and would be registered as similar by satellite surveillance. Furthermore, there is also the problem that warheads carrying chemical or biological substances would be designed to split, accentuating the problems of interception. More generally, there has been a major development in anti-satellite weaponry, tactics and doctrine, designed to counter satellite surveillance and interception, and this will continue. These developments challenge American hopes that a missile shield can offer invulnerability, and encourage consideration of plans that could not lead to deployment until a later date, for example for an Airborne Laser programme. This is designed to destroy enemy missiles in their boost phase, just after launching, rather than further into their trajectory. Possibly such a system would be less vulnerable to decoys, but its effectiveness is unclear.

In addition, as with Cold War atomic weaponry, we are dealing with the prospect of an attack for which there cannot be adequate defence trials. As with atomic weaponry, this does not prevent such trials, but the threat also encourages planning for pre-emptive strikes. In the Cold War, this led to the Anti-Ballistic Missile Treaty of 1972 which by banning the construction of a defensive shield left the USA and the USSR vulnerable to a missile attack. This was designed to discourage a first strike as there would be no effective defence against a counterstrike. The 1972 treaty served as the basis for further talks and encouraged restraint in the build-up of strategic-nuclear arsenals. It is far from clear that a similar prospect of negotiation, agreement and restraint exists with those powers currently defined as 'rogue' states. Furthermore, any process of negotiation would be far more complex as the number of participants would be greater than in the SALT talks.

It is appropriate to discuss the military threat from the 'rogue' states with reference to the Cold War, because there are several elements in common. One is an awareness of the need to plan for a war in which any success may itself probably be devastating to the victor as well as to the vanquished, even if the latter suffers far more. However, there are also important military differences. 'Rogue' states currently lack the intercontinental missile capability enjoyed by the Soviet Union and China during the Cold War, although they do increasingly possess a greater land mobility for their missiles. There were important developments in this direction in the 1980s, and, now and in the future, the firing mechanism and infrastructure required for long-range missiles are lighter and more mobile than hitherto. This created problems in the Gulf War – hunting the Iraqi Scuds – and these are likely to become greater in future conflicts.

As with Cold War atomic planning, but even more so given views on the maverick character of the leaders of 'rogue' states, this will increase pressure for a first strike option and thus for reliable surveillance and analysis of enemy dispositions, capability and plans. The reliability of current surveillance will need to be enhanced, in particular to scan underground positions.

If confrontations and conflicts were to be a matter of missile and counter-missile preparations and exchanges alone, then the role in such operations of ground troops might appear limited. It would essentially be that of protecting missile positions, although there would also be a role for specialist deep-penetration units sent to attack such positions. It is unclear how far this is a realistic scenario. To turn to specifics, 'rogue' states would be put under Western, i.e. largely American, pressure by the deployment offshore of warships with offensive missile and anti-missile capability. These ships would also serve as the base for airborne assault forces. If the latter can focus on attacking missile and communication centres, rather than on the difficult task of territorial control in the face of a hostile population, then they are likely to retain mobility and to make best use of their resources. However, it is likely that opponents would locate mobile missiles in heavily populated areas, and also fire them from there.

Thus search and destroy missions will face powerful political and military constraints. These will encourage the drive for a technology of detection, location and interception in flight. The search for such a technology is not new, and indeed was one of the principal features of research in the latter period of the Cold War. Heat signatures from rocket blasts were detected by satellites, and the rocket's trajectory rapidly evaluated. Land-based intercontinental rockets had ended American invulnerability, and this was followed by the development of hostile submarine forces capable of firing missiles from the American offshore.

From that perspective, the 'rogue' states scenario simply

increases the number of possible missile firers. This will be particularly the case as several of these states acquire submarines, as these overcome the constraints of national space, not least by vastly increasing an opponent's surveillance problems. Submarine forces are, however, more expensive to acquire and maintain than mobile land rocket launchers, and the West has a well-developed capability in anti-submarine warfare. Furthermore, the smaller number of units ensures that detection and destruction are proportionately more of a problem for the power using submarines. It is in the interests of the West that the entry costs to effective submarine capability remain high, and that submarine detection capability remains state of the art. Linked to this, it is in the interests of America that the geo-political concerns of 'rogue' states focus on near-neighbours, as this will ensure these dominate their military tasking. While Syria, Iraq, Iran and Libya might indeed desire an effective military capability able to threaten America, they will remain more concerned to acquire military assets that can threaten near-neighbours, such as each other and Israel. In part, this explains the threat from North Korea, because there the near-neighbourhood includes a substantial American force in South Korea.

The diffusion of advanced weaponry will increase the opportunity cost of fighting 'rogue' states. As was pointed out at the time, had Iraq or Serbia possessed atomic weaponry, then the response to the Gulf and Kosovo crises might have been very different. The same point could be made with reference to the successful international pressure on Indonesia in 1999 to withdraw its forces from East Timor. In addition, there are other forms of weaponry that would enhance the capability of 'rogue' states. One such is satellite information. The absence of this kept the Iraqis in the dark about the flanking movement of the US Third Army during Desert Storm in 1991.

A sense of vulnerability to universalist liberalism, in the form of renewed American assertiveness, has already encouraged strong pressures to develop nuclear capability. In the late

1990s, both India and Pakistan publicly tested nuclear weapons and developed long-distance missiles capable of carrying such weapons. They were far from alone in such preparations. In addition, the pharmacology of terror greatly expanded with developments in bacteriological and chemical weaponry.

These changes suggest that the future prospect for political globalism is bleak. However much a state or a group of states might dominate the power stakes, and however much diplomacy might resolve many problems, the costs of trying and failing to coerce a 'rogue' state are likely to rise to a point that encourages caution. This would not only be a *realpolitik* scenario; it would also be the politics of prudence that most military leaderships are apt to encourage. On the other hand, as the experience of the Vietnam War suggests, politicians, while inexperienced about military matters, listen only to the advice they wish to hear, and engage in promotion politics to ensure they receive this advice. Within the military, politicians can usually find those willing to offer it, and thus to advance or protect their own position.

Thus, it is possible that the politics of prudence will be countered by the imperatives of commitment. A good example of this is likely to occur in the Middle East. A scenario can readily be discerned in which Egypt is taken over by a more anti-Western leadership, whether 'fundamentalist' or not, and another Arab–Israeli war breaks out, possibly as a result of instability in Palestine, Jordan, Lebanon or Syria, or of the ambitions of a post-Assad and/or a post-Mubarrak government. This might not go well for Israel. Its airforce could be vulnerable to hand-held heat-seeking anti-aircraft weapons, its armour to similar anti-tank weaponry, and yet the prospect, or reality, of missile bombardment might draw the Israelis into a pre-emptive attack, as might the need to overcome their numerical inferiority by defeating their opponents in detail (separately).

The political pressure on the Americans to intervene would be considerable. There would be prudential restraints, not least military commitments elsewhere, for example in Korea and, perhaps, the Balkans, and the military advice might focus on the difficulty of the task, but it is likely that this would be ignored.

Given its resonance in American domestic politics, and long-standing American commitments, Israel might be regarded as an extreme case. Instead, it might be suggested that a second Iraqi invasion of Kuwait at a time of major American commitments elsewhere might be a more plausible litmus test. Whatever the politics, however, the problem of stronger (than hitherto) armaments on the part of the non-Western combatant will recur.

Furthermore, this is not simply a matter of a diffusion of advanced weaponry to states outside the first rank. There is also the problem of non-state organizations acquiring such weaponry. This is not new, and indeed was a feature of civil wars. However, then these were weapons at the disposal of proto-states, such as the Confederacy in the American Civil War, and of mass movements seeking to take over states, such as the Viet Minh. Now, advanced weapons can be acquired by movements that are far less numerous. The use of sarin nerve gas by Aum Shinrikyo, a Japanese sect, in an attack on the Tokyo underground in 1995, showed that lethal bacteriological and chemical weaponry could be made and used by non-state organizations. The limited effectiveness of the sect's attacks, despite the considerable resources at its disposal, was less striking than the attempt to widen the terrorist repertoire. As with firearms and earlier weapons, state monopolization of the means of violence proved to be limited. This was underlined by discussion about how a crude nuclear bomb could be fairly rapidly manufactured. This will not cease.

Such a situation did not mean that all weaponry could be easily replicated, or that it could be replicated in the quantities deployed by major powers. However, the potential capability of non-state players is a reminder of the danger of assessing and planning for conflict simply in state-to-state terms. The greater volatility of many of these players underlines the point.

The spread of advanced weaponry can be related to the continuing problems of counterinsurgency warfare. These will not diminish in future, and, indeed, may worsen because the greater machinery-to-manpower ratio of the modern military is of scant value for the militarized policing functions that controlling territory in such circumstances entails. Thus, the Angolan government uses MiG 23 bombers, helicopter gunships, tanks and heavy artillery against the UNITA rebels, but finds it difficult to contain their far-flung guerrilla attacks.

It is easy to be pessimistic about the likely consequences. In many respects, the brutality referred to as ethnic cleansing may become more common as states struggle to control hostile populations, while guerrillas terrorize alleged collaborators. Both processes can be seen in the Angolan civil war. Conversely, the problems that guerrilla operations encounter, including the supply of adequate munitions, may well encourage terrorism, instead of such operations, as well as a level of non co-operation that makes government difficult. The nature of state response to sustained opposition will reflect ideologies and circumstances, but it is likely to be violent in those states that possess authoritarian political systems, a list that includes most of Africa and South-West Asia. Thus, the military will find the maintenance of government power its first obligation in many states. While in some countries, this will be planned for with due care to civilian rights and even with the use of non-lethal weaponry, in others there will be a descent into brutal thuggery. The politicization of the military and the militarization of politics will be a synergy that it is all too difficult to overcome. This undercuts any optimism about a demilitarization dividend from reduced international tension.

To turn to operational factors, the difficulties of dealing with a hostile population will be a factor both for 'developed' and for 'less developed' military powers. At one level, they indicate the limitations of any sharp differentiation of military from civilian opponents. In particular, the value of successful manoeuvre warfare – the dislocation of opposing military structures – will be compromised by the problems of destroying units and, even more, controlling territory. The latter will indicate the continued vitality of the defence at one level at least.

This is important because not only Western technology but also its operational doctrine presupposes that success will flow from the seizure and maintenance of the initiative. Western forces are both trained and organized for this, and their structure and ethos are particularly appropriate for such operations. Indeed, Western military theory argues that the willingness to entrust decisions to low-level commanders encourages a fluidity that is the enabler of mobility, providing operational and tactical advantages over the products of more centralized political-social systems. This may work for the penetration battle, but war should involve a successful exit-strategy as well as an effective entry one, and it is unclear that the military and political consequences have been adequately considered and integrated into planning.

Looking ahead, it is possible to see the character and processes of future conflict as very varied. This will represent a continuation of present trends, and it is difficult to foresee any revolutionary shift. The latter tend to be envisaged in terms of new weaponry, but, as already suggested, that confuses the means of conflict with its ends. It also neglects the extent to which innovations in weapons, tactics and strategy are rapidly diffused and/or are quickly matched by counter-weapons, tactics and strategy. There is no reason to believe that the same will not continue to be the case. Thus, for example, as satellites are developed both for surveillance and as weapons platforms, so anti-satellite capability will be enhanced. This will take the form both of killer satellites and of ground-based weaponry, jamming and evasion devices and practices.

The desire to control the battlefield and reduce or manage risk appeals to many facets of current Western culture, not least the absence of fatalism and the belief in planning. It also reflects the role of planning staffs, the nature of peacetime preparedness, and the attempt to integrate planning into conflict as a continual process. However, it is less than probable that peacetime planning will 'work' as intended other than for offensive forces, with overwhelming power, launching very short conflicts. This does not mean that planning is without value, but, rather, that it cannot replace risk and must not be used to encourage the notion of risk-free operations.

Furthermore, it is necessary to understand the weakness of Western powers in managing exits from conflict. This is a function of excessive confidence in the 'total victory' that technological disparities are supposed to guarantee, Western incomprehension in negotiating with different world views, and cultural habits and institutional orientations within the military that can make it difficult to accept limited victory.

A true military 'revolution' would entail, for example, a shift back towards widespread military service and/or a willingness to inflict and, still more, suffer heavy casualties. An attempt to create a global military presence in order to enforce an international order, and thus provide a different context for 'just' wars, would also be revolutionary. There are no signs of any such changes. The enthusiasm with which commentators detect military revolutions needs to be contained.

5 Conclusion

> We have regional dangers and the threat of aggression by hostile states against our friends and allies and interests in key regions. I'm speaking specifically, of course, about Southwest Asia and Northeast Asia. We have the possibility of regional instability and also failed states . . . We do not see or expect a regional power or a peer competitor for the next 10 or 15 years, but we have to prepare for that possibility certainly in the years beyond.
>
> William Cohen, Secretary of Defense, 'Quadrennial Defense Review' (1997)

In its fundamentals, war changes far less frequently and significantly than most people appreciate. This is not simply because it involves a constant – the willingness of organized groups to kill and, in particular, to risk death – but also because the material culture of war, which tends to be the focus of attention, is less important than its social, cultural and political contexts and enablers. These contexts explain the purposes of military action, the nature of the relationship between the military and the rest of society, and the internal structures and ethos of the military. Having 'high-tech', the focus of much discussion about the future of war, is not the same as winning particular wars, and, anyway, does not delimit the nature of conflict.

An awareness of the limitations of 'high-tech' does not, however, provide much guidance for the composition of future force structures, although it is valuable for an understanding of their likely use and capability. Instead, it is helpful to have an understanding of the destabilizing character of change. Change, indeed, is integral to the nature of the modern world. It would be amazing if the twentieth century, which saw astonishing developments in capability and conflict, was succeeded by a century of stasis. There is no reason in modern culture or scientific capability to envisage such a shift, and the notion of modernity as a constantly changing presence and aspiration will continue. If anything, current trends indicate an acceleration of change as innovations in genetics, neuroscience and other fields proliferate through the rapid global communications system.

Acknowledging the role of change is not the same as stating the potency of all changes, but to focus on this role, and concentrating, at this point, on weaponry, rather than doctrine, one can say that it is likely that, at the high end of the conflict spectrum, the weapons and weapons systems that dominate at the present moment will both remain central for probably two decades and then will be superseded. New weapons will need to combine firepower and mobility characteristics, the basic needs of modern combat, but will try to lessen the frictions associated with use. Issues of durability, vulnerability and damage through use are all important.

To look further ahead, beyond a 40-year span, is to consider the possibility of discovering and using new properties of matter, or, at least, of particular materials, or ranges of spectrums. It is also likely that more effort will be devoted to creating effective means to disorientate the minds of opponents. Information jamming will not be restricted to attacks on material systems. The creation of precision disorientation weapons may be linked to future advances in the understanding of the chemistry and mechanics of the brain. The ability to affect these in a predictable fashion will be developed in medical science, and then there will be a search for military application. In turn, this will drive a search for counter measures.

Such suggestions imply that there will be further discussion about the 'laws of war'. There may well be a sense that brain-interfering and sense-altering weaponry is unacceptable, but it is also likely to be seen as an acceptable alternative to physical destruction.

Looking further to the future, it is possible that cloning will be used to produce more 'disposable' soldiery. Genetic engineering, however, is likely to be more constrained than developments in the machinization of war that lead towards more effective robotic soldiers. In 2000, a Roboguard, a handgun mounted on a motorized arm, was produced in Thailand. The weapon can be programmed to fire automatically as soon as a target is selected. It does not require a human aimer as it uses a video camera, infrared sensors and a laser sight. Such a weapon could easily be made mobile or given greater firepower. It is probable that this invention will be pursued.

An awareness of the prospect of continued radical change in weaponry will affect investment in the platforms from which weapons are fired. More generally, there will be a problem of continued investment demands. These will affect all powers, but their ability to respond will vary greatly, and this will help determine ongoing and subsequent absolute and relative capability. Issues will include not only wealth, but also established patterns of taxation and expenditure. Thus, states that have heavy commitments in social welfare may find it difficult to match the expenditure of those that do not. Linked to this, but not coterminous, there is the question of the relationship between the wealth of a society and the ability of the government to dominate and control resource use. This involves not only taxation levels, but also the degree of state direction of the economy. Thus, those governments that may be able to spend the highest percentage of national resources on military preparations are authoritarian states, followed by non-authoritarian societies with a low level of social welfare, and, lastly, those with a high level of social welfare. In crude modern terms, this typology is represented by China, the USA and the European Union.

In the past, it was possible to argue that this was not too threatening a prospect, as authoritarian systems with their planning systems and arbitrary policies were inherently inefficient in terms of the requirements of capitalism for processes by which resources were best allocated in order to ensure productivity and growth. This involved more than economic processes. The USA is far more flexible than autocratic societies, both in considering past and present and in searching for advantage in the future.

A society like the USA, which is open to talent, and without a caste-like social structure, a rigid ideology, or an autocratic government, should be better able to respond to the challenges of the future, than a society affected by one or more of these characteristics. In military terms, this responsiveness includes being able to respond to the need for initiative in doctrine, strategy, tactics and weaponry. In both World War II and the Cold War, the Americans were more successful than their opponents in encouraging and organizing a systemic productivity that provided a massive build-up of an effective military without jeopardizing the domestic economy; instead, there was a positive synergy.

It is unclear whether the future will be comparably benign, and this is crucial because American power politics depends on retaining a world-leading capability, while American public culture with its moralism and self-confidence has little tolerance of the idea of restraints imposed by others. Although the search for national victory leaves many intellectuals uncomfortable, it retains wide support in American public culture.

America is at present, and in the foreseeable future, the sole power able to set convincing limits to the aspirations of expansionist regimes and to give force to definitions of 'rogue' statedom. This is important to the political health of the entire world. A move from American great-powerdom to hegemony by another state, for example China, or, more plausibly, to a condition in which there is no such hegemony, would be of more than abstract interest, and would mark more than simply a turn in the cyclical great-power theories of political scientists. America's lack of interest in territorial aggrandizement and the absence of racialism and religious intolerance from American public culture will ensure that American global policy is benign in terms of liberal anti-authoritarian standards. Such a comment will surprise those used to the active or latent anti-Americanism of much world public debate on international relations, but, in practice, America is more benign than might be expected from an alternative, which, at present, means an authoritarian, great power. The argument that America's political and civil culture makes its global influence benign in a significant sense will, for many, be a counter-intuitive argument, but such arguments are important if we are to understand the complex and unpredictable context within which future conflicts will occur, and the difficulty of making judgements. Other counter-intuitive points that need stressing include the possibility that economic growth can increase the likelihood of conflict, and that 'losers' in war can reverse the verdict by other means.

Relative benignity does not mean that American power will not continue to support regimes and policies that fail to match up to the aspirations of American public culture, as it has done in Latin America. Yet, in part, this is a matter of the global representation of hegemonic power: it is not always, indeed usually, possible to choose allies that accord with one's ideals.

It is difficult to envisage the replacement of American hegemony without either war or the creation of another leading military power. If the former entailed an equivalent to the Vietnam War, it might be followed by a withdrawal from American interventionalism that left the world without a hegemonic power. This is more plausible than the creation of another power capable of matching the present position of the USA, but such a remark may well underrate future volatility in world politics and a consequent willingness to support or accept a new hegemon.

The leading candidate is China, but, if so, it is unclear whether this would be a revisionist China seeking to remould the politics of part or much of the world, or, instead, a state willing to dominate while accepting the constraints of non-interventionism, specifically the sovereignty of other states. In addition, it is unclear whether the process by which China might achieve objectives at the expense of its near-neighbours may not involve a degree of conflict that ensures that Chinese great-power status is both distinctly militaristic and continually vigilant in the face of perceived revisionist tendencies on the part of states that have been defeated.

Chinese military power will continue to differ from that of the USA for geo-political and social reasons. The first will ensure that naval power will be less important to Chinese force structure and doctrine. In the short term, the instability of Russia and Central Asia will accentuate this, but, in the long term, lengthy borders with hostile neighbours will ensure it. Secondly, Chinese forces will continue to have a lower standard of living than their American counterparts and thus fewer logistical demands. This will be important to their comparative manoeuvrability. The demands of American forces and of their weaponry are such that the logistical tail is a major constraint, as well as providing a vulnerable link, open to malfunction, or to attack by advanced weaponry or low-tech guerrilla opposition.

The importance of the geo-political point above is a reminder that even symmetrical warfare does not involve conflict between identical forces: even if weapons are similar, force structures are not. There is a dependence of doctrine, technology and force structure on strategy, and of the latter on political concerns, that must not be forgotten.

Whatever the nature of Chinese power in the future, it is likely that major states will continue to have to plan for symmetrical and asymmetrical conflict, and for high- and low-tech operations. Yet it is also necessary, when looking to the future, to accept that such categories are malleable and may indeed require continual re-definition. The last century, and also the last decade, underline the extent of unpredictability in human affairs. Repeatedly, predictions have been proved wrong, both about international relations and about domestic developments. There is no reason to believe that the future will be any different. On the contrary, the pace of change is likely to remain high and will probably become even greater as the normative value of past and present arrangements declines in nearly all human societies.

Conceptual flexibility is important if a tasks- or threats-based approach to force structures and doctrine is taken, rather than, as is often tempting, a capabilities-based approach; in other words if the focus is on the tasks the military may be given and the threats they will confront, rather than simply building up their capability, in particular by acquiring advanced weapons systems. The problem of preparing for the last war, a charge frequently made against the military, can in part be clarified by emphasizing the diversity of military tasks and the unpredictability of the manner in which these tasks present themselves in crises and conflicts.

The complexity of military tasking leads to an inevitable tension between politicians and public, who seek to have a military able to take on all tasks, and militaries who point out the difficulty of achieving adequate flexibility with limited resources, necessitating the sophisticated management of priorities. Looking to the future, this prioritization will be most effective if it can escape the constraints of individual service interests, in short if overall forces structures are more than the sum of compartmentalized services. This flexibility will in part depend upon political support and direction.

It is possible to envisage many changes over the next century. War might be dehumanized by entrusting combat to computers, thus, apparently, taking machinization to its logical conclusion. Alternatively, the vulnerability of human societies to environmental damage could be exploited in a systematic form. In short, there is no reason to believe that the capability of war for adaptation and major change will diminish.

Yet, alongside these ideas, it is more than likely that standard aims will continue and that familiar problems will persist. How can states control dissident groups? How can they guarantee security in an unstable world? How can they use military capability to achieve their objectives short of the unpredictable hazards of war? It is difficult to feel that any of these issues will change. The globalist aspirations of 1945 and 1990 seem defeated by the durability of differences within human society, as much as by the continued centrality of the sovereign state and the lack across much of the world of stable civil societies. One prediction seems safe. Talk of the obsolescence, even end, of war will prove misplaced, and will be mocked by the rictus on the face of the dead.

Index

DATE DUE